# Recovering the Sacred Center

"Here is a book that will make you think. It is useful in helping serious Christians not only to keep up but also to stay ahead in the struggle to keep the church relevant in our changing world."
—*Millard Fuller, Founder and President, Habitat for Humanity International*

"In the thicket of scrub-oak manuals for improving congregations, this book is a sequoia. Rigorous theology, superb insights, and powerful anecdotes make this an exceptional guide for transforming congregational life."
—*Walter Wink, Professor of Biblical Interpretation, Auburn Theological Seminary*

"Howard Friend invites pastors and congregational leaders to recover the soul of their church, to nurture it and allow its transformation into fresh ministries of inreach and outreach."
—*Robert Raines, author, speaker, activist*

"No pious platitudes or churchy fluff, this is the real thing—authentic spiritual formation which enables the people of God to move the church of God forward while it is buffeted by the winds of change."
—*Bishop Barbara Harris, The Episcopal Diocese of Massachusetts*

"This book will help you rethink as you revitalize!"
—*Peter L. Steinke, Editor, New Creation*

"I heartily recommend this book as a valuable study resource for pastors and lay leaders in any church."
—*Richard Stoll Armstrong,*
*Ashenfelter Professor of Ministry and Evangelism Emeritus*

"Friend challenges pervasive ideas and persuasively resurfaces the notion that the revitalization of the church can be defined by faithfulness to a congregation's deeply considered vision of what it means to be authentically Christian. His work transcends the trendy technique-driven advice that is so readily available today."
—*Cindy Crowner, Director, Kirkridge Center*

"For those who are frustrated and often immobilized by the lack of vitality of their church in the face of the tremendous challenges of a changing world, Howard Friend offers an exciting new way ahead."
—*Richard Shaull, professor, author, activist*

"*Recovering the Sacred Center* will contribute mightily to the revitalization of many kinds of community within the Church at large."
—*Rev. John Neville, OSC, Provincial of the Crosier Fathers and Brothers*

"A perfect antidote to the 'functional atheism' that leads congregations to behave as if God didn't exist."
—*Ed White, Senior Consultant, Alban Institute*

"*Recovering the Sacred Center* is the natural and exceptional fruit of several decades of pastoral leadership, congregational partnership, and spiritual exploration."
—*Manfred T. Brauch, Professor of Biblical Theology,*
*Eastern Baptist Theological Seminary*

"Howard Friend provides you with theological and biblical resources to map your own journeys into mission."
—*Thomas A. Michael, Department of Management, Rowan University*

"Recently, at the end of a five-day retreat, a group of executives were asked what is the overriding need of the day. The unanimous answer was: to rediscover and celebrate the sacred center. How timely is Howard Friend's book, which explains trenchantly just how to do that."
—*Fr. William McNamara, Founder and Abbot, Spiritual Life Institute*

# Recovering the Sacred Center
## Church Renewal from the Inside Out

Howard E. Friend Jr.

Judson Press ® Valley Forge

Inquiries for the author may be addressed to: Parish Empowerment Network, 698 Spruce Drive, West Chester, PA 19382; hfriend@prodigy.net.

Cover design by Paul Hesser and Bo Bartlett. Text diagrams by Herman DeJong.

Library of Congress Cataloging-in-Publication Data

Friend, Howard E., Jr.
  Recovering the sacred center : church renewal from the inside out / Howard E. Friend Jr.
    p. cm.
  ISBN 0-8170-1274-5 (pbk. : alk. paper)
  1. Church renewal. 2. Church renewal—United States—Case studies.
I. Title.
BV600.2.F72 1998
262'.001'7—dc21                               98-13818

Printed in the U.S.A.
08 07 06 05 04 03 02 01
5 4 3 2

*For*
BETSY
*my confidante and friend*
*my companion on the journey*
*my partner in ministry*
*my love and joy*
*and*
DAVID *and* LINDA, DRAKE *and* TODD
ERIK *and* GRISELDA
*sons, daughters-in-law, and grandsons*
*the circle at my sacred center*

# Contents

## Part Three

# Foreword

In this book you will have a remarkable opportunity for a guided tour of the rich and mysterious world of religious faith. What lies ahead is land we in churches find familiar—the land in which individuals and families find meaning in the ordinary things of life. I say "ordinary," but Howard Friend opens the ordinary stuff of life to the deep dimensions within it. This book helps us feel the difference between a conversation and an encounter, between a decision and a commitment, between a job and a vocation. In other words, this is a three-dimensional exploration of life that most people live in two dimensions only.

It is this third dimension that people of our society are hunting for in what even the *Wall Street Journal* suggests may be a new awakening to the spiritual dimension of life. Bookshelves cannot be stocked fast enough with the latest wisdom about "spirituality," with the latest "How to Get Better" book (usually in two versions, one with God and one without), or with intrigue about angels or vampires. As a society, we seem to be starving for the latest spiritual fad that promises a better way. Anxiety about the larger, deeper dimensions of life that we all know in our hearts must be there leads us to fruitless pursuit of charlatans of the spirit as well as to those who simply try to shock our senses.

This is a book about a different way, one that takes seriously the wisdom of thousands of years of religious experience and is based on the structures of spiritual adventure developed in four millennia of experience with the God of Abraham and Sarah, and in two millennia as companions to the story and the living presence of the one who died on a cross.

This book also takes very seriously the fact that much of that wisdom has lost its hold on those living at the edge of the twenty-first century. And it is because we have lost our sense of connection to the true center that we are patsies for any con artist with a new spiritual shtick.

The land to be explored here is familiar land. Many of us traverse middle-class life that most mainline church people find familiar—people struggling with job pressures in a world where jobs used to be lifelong, hungry for friendships in a depersonalized society, searching for answers for themselves that they can also pass on to their children. As people who are not poor, we are not sure how we should relate to the worlds of poverty.

In particular, Friend focuses the questions of life through the work of the religious congregation—a place he sees as the arena in which those struggles and that search can be carried out. Those who are sacramentalists among us can appreciate his understanding of congregational life as the outward and visible sign of a deep spiritual reality. But by focusing on this spiritual reality, Friend is not saying that the real stuff of life and of congregations is sucked up into some amorphous, romantic fuzz, like the music at the end of a movie that signals everybody is going to live happily ever after. It is not that kind of spirituality at all. It is a spiritual territory in which people have fights and hurt each other. It is a world where those who pray to live happily sometimes end up divorced. It is a territory in which people sitting on a committee can be at complete loggerheads with one another and where petulance and self-aggrandizement are alive.

The gift of this book is that it sees such ugliness as real but is not overwhelmed by it. This book sees in and through these sometimes unsatisfying dynamics the power of God seeking to touch and heal. This book is not about a hope that is in the by-and-by but a hope that begins now with actual people doing things with the people they know and care about. It is for real.

At the heart of this book is the conviction that each of us is called to be in relationship to the sacred center and that everything else depends on that. We find also the conviction that each congregation can help us search for our own center as the body faces the need to discern its own corporate sacred center. In this book you will be helped to explore all this uncharted country and you will be invited to begin or continue your pilgrimage through it. You will need undaunted courage—what has always been needed by those venturing into new lands.

Your tour guide is Howard Friend, Presbyterian. He is a bit of a maverick in his own denomination, one who has often strayed to work with those in other denominations, one who has developed the ability to ask questions and push the edges in every religious community he meets.

But you are also guided by Howard Friend, educator. Perhaps no characteristic of Howard is clearer in this book than his compulsion to learn and to design ways for others to learn. He believes in the potential for learning in every situation, even every dilemma. He reminds me of Reuel Howe's admonition, "Anything that happens is grist for the mill of learning."

You will probably most enjoy Howard Friend, raconteur. What a wealth of stories—some funny, some grim, some open-ended. It is the stories that carry us along, illustrating the points, pointing beyond themselves, sometimes exploding with things we had not known before. The stories bring a warmth and wisdom, the sense of real people making real decisions.

You will also appreciate Howard Friend, pioneer. Pioneers blaze trails so others can follow. You will find many options laid out here, along with landmarks and advice about what to do when you get lost.

With any luck, though, you will also find what I found—Howard Friend, companion on the way. Howard is very conscious of those of us who share this journey with him. He moves ahead, but he also seeks to learn from us, his companions, and values whoever we are and whatever we bring.

I deeply believe there is a sacred center to which we are all related and that the sacred center searches for us long before we are conscious of the need to seek it out. This book is a guide for us who seek to be companions on the way.

*Loren B. Mead*

# Preface

Some years ago, as I drove each day to my office at Gladwyne Presbyterian Church, I passed three different houses in the process of renovation. Each was of historic vintage, and each was in the demolition phase of the work. In all three projects the contractors could not be certain as they began the work just how much would need to be torn away before restoration could begin.

One house required that only a few boards be removed before solid, unrotted timbers were exposed. Reconstruction began quickly. The second house presented a different story. The clapboard siding had to be completely removed, the face of the house supported by temporary posts, while many of the interior structural members were torn away as well. Reconstruction was delayed for weeks while the painstaking work of preparation proceeded. The third house demanded the most drastic work. It had to be dismantled down to the foundation. After demolition only the fireplace and parts of two walls remained standing. Rebuilding was delayed for months while debris was separated from salvageable material. The house was completely reconstructed.

A year later a lovely home stood on each site. Cars were parked in the driveways, new shrubbery had been carefully planted, and children played in the yards. Each project had demanded different amounts of work, patience, and, no doubt, money.

In the past four years I have worked as a consultant with more than forty churches. Over the past thirty-two years I have worked as a pastor with five congregations and through pastoral colleagues have been exposed to hundreds more. I know well the everyday life of parishes. Many need renovation. Like the first of those three houses, in some cases the work required will be minimal. In other cases—the majority I am guessing—it may be extensive. We will not know until we begin.

This book is an invitation and a challenge to begin the work. It will demand hearty commitment and high determination, constant prayer and alert discernment, tireless effort and openness to divine grace. This is not a one-size-fits-all template for congregational renewal. This is a faith-based, spiritually grounded approach. Each congregation must discern its own unique calling. Only recovering the sacred center—of individuals and congregations—can lead to reinvention of the church.

I speak from my experience—as a pastor, professor, workshop leader, pastoral psychotherapist, consultant, and writer. These pages are filled with anecdotes from dozens of local congregations, but more than any other single parish, you will hear most about Gladwyne Presbyterian Church. Each of these churches, though primarily Gladwyne Church, has been my mentor. Theirs have been the stories from which I have learned what I know.

In part 1, I introduce what I perceive to be the crisis and challenge facing the church and thus the choices we are called upon to make. I introduce the cornerstone metaphor of the book—recovering the sacred center. In part 2, I introduce a way of thinking and speaking theologically that encompasses the idea of sacred center. In part 3, I address leadership, organization, and governance in transforming congregations, the way sacred center manifests in church admini- stration. And finally, in a conclusion I narrate twenty-three years of mission and outreach at Gladwyne Presbyterian Church in Gladwyne, Pennsylvania. This case study shows both how the principles of this book evolved and what they look like in action.

You may find it tempting at times to jump ahead to what may seem at first glance to be the more practical themes of later chapters. I hope you will resist that temptation. You may find yourself trying to rush through these pages, to read the book on a long plane ride or to finish it in a couple of sittings. I hope you will not do that either. I write at times quite philosophically and theologically; at other times, quite personally and reflectively. I have not hesitated to share my perspectives and biases, my worldview and vision. But I would find either your wholehearted agreement or your total dismissal equally unfortunate. I hope you will receive my ideas as grist for the mill for your own reflection and dialogue.

As a parish pastor for over thirty years, I am no stranger to the joys and frustrations, the hopes and discouragements of local church leadership. Those decades forged in me a deep, steady, and passionate commitment to the local church. Individual Christians and congregations can behave poorly. People looking for a church home may find countless depressed, lifeless, spiritually dry congregations. Denominations seem bent on self-destruction. Critics of the church, the cynics and pessimists, are persuasive. Yet I am convinced that local churches can be vital and life-giving communities where spiritual life can unfold and flourish. I hope you will find in these pages strength and wisdom for your journey, be it personal or congregational. I encourage you to consider moving on only after you have found five or six others in your congregation who will read this book with you. If these ideas are to become generative in the life of your congregation, they are better brought forward by a team of people. New ideas brought to a church by individual laypeople are often rebuffed. New ideas brought by clergy are often received cordially, with apparent interest and cooperation. But they have little long-term impact. In contrast, a team of people with a new idea can become leaven in the congregation. So, if you are a pastor, find four or five lay leaders from your congregation to join you. If you are a layperson, ask your pastor and four or five other laity to be your companions.

I was once a participant in a leadership skills and team-building exercise called orienteering. Divided into groups of five, we began at a common starting point with instructions to make our way to a common destination. There were, however, endless possible routes to take. The challenge to each group was to map the way. Each was given a pack of basic tools, a compass, and a pat on the back from the instructor.

You and I have a common starting point—a desire to provide leadership for the renewal of the church. We have a common destination—a renewed, revitalized, perhaps reinvented church. But there is no right way to arrive at our destination. All churches and their leaders must draw their own maps, plan their own route, and travel their own course. I offer a pack, a compass, and a pat on the back.

# Acknowledgments

It does take a village—to write a book! I have never lingered very long with the acknowledgment pages of books I have read, except when I have had some dim hope that I might find myself among those named and appreciated. But now it is very clear to me how profoundly important, to the author, at least, these pages are.

Betsy comes first: sweetheart since we met at senior high church camp, wife of thirty-six years, lover and companion, colleague and friend. Our sons, David and Erik, are clearly next, with their wives, Linda and Griselda, and grandson, Drake: only the inner circle really counts. My dad, Howard, who has known me and loved me the longest; my mom, Mary, who taught me, by her quiet Catholic devotion, the essence of true ecumenicity; my mother, Marjorie, whose death when I was fourteen resulted in my spending years struggling with grief but eventually released my compassion and set my course in ministry.

A bounty of faces from Gladwyne Presbyterian Church, too many to name, are the threads that weave meaning and wonder through these pages. And I am thankful for many more from Montauk, Honey Brook, Union, and Trinity Presbyterian Churches, where I also served as pastor. These congregations loved and nurtured me, affirmed and supported me, and far too often were forced to tolerate me. I was in many ways a slow learner.

I lean back in my chair and a wonderful collage of names and faces stream by—teachers and mentors, colleagues and partners, family and friends: David and Judd; Ken, George, and Ken; Dave and Gail; Susie, Mark, and Rya; Arnie, Newt, and Bob; Barbara and

Terry; David, Doug, and Bruce. And others who will keep coming to mind long after I have completed this list.

This book is truly a collaborative effort; writing has not come easily to me. Thanks to those who read and critiqued the various editions of this text: Jim, Bruce, Doug, Tom, Bob, Julie, Morris, Ruth, Susan, Barry, Jerry, Terry, Barbara, and especially Bob Sherman, Mark Robbins, George Bustard, and Ruth Ann Schlarbaum. And, just when I was losing heart, an editor who understood what I was trying to say, handled my fragile ego gently, worked artfully with the text, and helped me bring it home: Randy Frame. Beth Gaede was a masterful copyeditor. Hal Rast, Kristy Arnesen Pullen, Tina Edginton, and Victoria McGoey at Judson Press provided encouragement, guidance, and support throughout the process.

The ride back to Delhi from a day at Agra and the Taj Mahal in the fall of 1993 was harrowing. Anything and everything clog the highways in India. Afraid to look through the windshield as we careened through the darkness, I turned toward the backseat to chat with Betsy and the couple with whom we shared the car and driver. "Why are you here in India?" I asked, trying to distract us from our anxiety. "We're writing a book," came the reply. "Really," I replied, "I'm writing a book too."

Where did that come from? I thought to myself, because I was not writing a book, though as of that moment I was. God works in strange ways. I am always a bit annoyed at people who say that they feel "called" to this or that. It seems arrogant and presumptuous. Yet from that moment I felt just that—called to write this book. So I want to express my gratitude to God for calling me to this work and sustaining me through what has seemed at times an endless process.

In more ways than I could count or find words to express, I am very grateful.

*Part One*

# Crisis, Challenge, and Choice
## A Call to the Sacred Center

In his book *All That Is Solid Melts into Air: An Experience of Modernity,* Marshall Berman defines modernism as

> a struggle to make ourselves at home in a constantly changing world. . . . To be modern is to experience personal and social life as a maelstrom, to find one's world and oneself in perpetual disintegration and renewal, trouble and anguish, ambiguity and contradiction: to be part of a universe in which all that is solid melts into air.[1]

Individuals and organizations, Christians and congregations, experience that provocative definition every day: "all that is solid melts into air." In the long sweep of history we do, indeed, live in a tumultuous, rapidly changing, seemingly chaotic world. Once reliable certainties are collapsing. Ours is an era of paradigm shifting.

Imagine the Empire State Building, with a telephone book perched on its radio tower, a nickel on the phone book, and a postage stamp—glue-side up—on the nickel. The Empire State Building represents the five million years since the first humanoids stood upright and began to fathom life on earth. The phone book represents the five thousand years since the dawn of rudimentary history keeping and written language. The nickel represents the five-plus decades of my lifetime. The postage stamp represents the past five years. And the glue on the stamp represents the year I have spent writing this book.

A not insignificant level of knowledge and life mastery accumulated in that first five million years. By 3000 B.C., metals had been alloyed both for implements of warfare and agricultural tools, and innovative farming techniques had spread across Europe to central Africa. Basic architectural forms had been mastered allowing two-tiered buildings and the construction of temples. Animals had been domesticated. And basic political, economic, social, and religious structure had emerged.

It took only five thousand years, the phone book perched on the radio tower, to double that accumulated knowledge. By 1940 much of what we call the modern age was firmly established. Research spurred by the war effort soon yielded nuclear fusion, global communication technology, dramatic medical advances, and sophisticated travel options, including jet aviation.

It took just fifty years, the nickel on the phone book, to double accumulated knowledge again and less than five years to double it still again. We approach a time when in less than a given calendar year, the glue on the postage stamp, we will double knowledge again and more.

This era of profound change has outdistanced personal and organizational ability to respond on every front. It is like navigating permanent white water, suggests social critic Pete Vaill. Instability abounds. The very ground beneath us seems to be shifting. We hover at times near some psychic red line. Change, once viewed as intermittent, now seems constant. Indeed, the nature of change itself is changing.

Part 1, "Crisis, Challenge, and Choice," although fully aware of all that is disruptive in our time, offers a call to realistic hope and to a bold adventure. We are in need of new directions, of new paradigm pioneers. This is a time of crisis, of danger and opportunity (chapter 1). We must face it with courage and honesty. Although we may not be able to shift that reality dramatically, we can choose how to respond. My proposal is to recover the sacred center (chapter 2).

*Chapter One*

# Wanted:
# New Paradigm Pioneers

Much has been written in the last twenty years about paradigm shifting. We are surrounded, one can persuasively argue, by paradigm shifts in every sector—medicine, psychotherapy, technology, nutrition, transportation, telecommunications, and education, just to name a few. We must add church to this list.

A paradigm ("pattern") is a mental framework, a basic worldview, a way of understanding, explaining, and interacting with reality, often largely unconscious, but held as if it were self-evident and absolute. Paradigm shifts may actually occur decades before the new reality fully enters everyday consciousness. Even after the paradigm shift has begun, people and institutions continue to behave with old-paradigm assumptions. People are continually surprised and bewildered by disappointing and negative results, though these outcomes are both predictable and inevitable. Old-paradigm assumptions enable us to cope only poorly, surely not creatively, in a new-paradigm reality.

Futurist Joel Barker has explored nuances of paradigm shifting and offers a provocative distinction between what he calls "paradigm shifters" and "paradigm pioneers."[1] Paradigm *shifters*, he suggests, look incisively and insightfully at the world. They name and track dynamics of profound change, predicting challenges that will ensue. More than observers and analysts, they may be instigators and collaborators in paradigm shifting as well. Paradigm *pioneers*, on the other hand, are those who dare in the midst of

paradigm shifting to venture forth into newly opened terrain. Like
Columbus, they venture past the edges of existing maps, sail
uncharted waters, and seek the undiscovered and wander through
the unexplored.

This transformational work demands courage and offers exhila-
ration. This is not a journey for the fainthearted. These pioneers will
need to muster determination and stamina. At the same time, this
journey invites a sense of lightheartedness and welcomes a spirit of
playfulness. Indeed, this serious and urgent work is best undertaken
by those who do not take themselves too seriously.

## Recovering the Sacred Center: A Wake-Up Call

Thomas Merton, a contemplative monk and mystic who died in
1968, spoke with remarkable incisiveness to our time. He wrote that
personal and spiritual transformation means detaching and drawing
back from what he calls our "false self," falling through the "center
of ourselves," then emerging as the "true self."[2] Old Testament
scholar Walter Brueggemann observes that the biblical people of
God were continually born and reborn "from within."[3] Saxophonist
Charlie Parker said simply, "If it's not in your heart, then it's not in
your horn." Each of these people, widely separated in space and
time, concurs that transformation comes from a willingness to be
deeply and profoundly renewed from the inside out, to recover the
sacred center.

Too many books about congregational development and parish
leadership focus on the outside rather than the inside. More cosmetic than substantive—filled with methods, strategies, models,
and procedures to be applied by local churches—these books focus
on symptoms rather than substance. Generic templates for fostering
church growth, instilling congregational liveliness, or restructuring
church organization engender false hope and encourage passivity,
even laziness, on the part of congregational leaders. These strategies produce short-lived effectiveness, if they are effective at all.

Renewal from within requires a clear sense of self-identity. This
was concisely stated by a Swedish Lutheran bishop to a group of
church leaders as they faced the advancing Nazi threat earlier in
this century. His answer to the question, What are we to do? speaks

to us as well: "First we must know who we *are*, and then we will know what to do."

What most often prompts a church to call the Parish Empowerment Network, the group of professionals with whom I do consulting work, is some variation of the questions, What should we do? and How should we do it? My typical reply is, "These are good questions, but they're questions number two and three. What is God calling you to be? What is the mission you have prayerfully discerned? What is your sense of identity as a people? These are the questions to ask first."

The visible church—its architecture, worship, program life, and organizational structure—may radically change, taking on dramatically new and different forms. But the invisible church—its deepest identity, its basic calling, its divine intention—can only be discerned and (re)discovered.

And this work of discernment and discovery takes time. I often find myself saying to clients and students, "You are thinking in terms of weeks and months. Think in terms of years and decades!"

A story from my childhood perfectly illustrates the condition of many churches. For my sixth birthday I received from my grandmother a goldfish I named Harvey. After school I would pull a dining room chair up to the bay window where we put Harvey's bowl and carefully pinch in just the right amount of food. As I watched him swim in the shimmering afternoon sun, something caught my eye. Harvey always swam around his bowl in the same direction, in the same path, at the same speed—an inch inside the rim of the bowl, an inch below the surface of the water, round and round like the hands of a clock. If I stirred the water with my finger, or pinched in the food along a different trail, he would change direction—but only for a minute. Then back he would go to his predictable, boring pattern.

When Harvey's bowl turned cloudy, Grandma announced, "It's time to change his water. We'll fetch him out with that little net we brought from the pet store and put him in the spaghetti pot while we clean his bowl." I had a better idea. "Let's put Harvey in the bathtub while we clean his bowl," I suggested. Harvey could swim from one end of the tub to the other, back and forth, along the bottom and across the top. "He'll have a terrific time," I said.

Grandma carried Harvey's bowl up the stairs to the bathroom,

eased it over the edge of the tub, gently lowered it to the surface of
the water, and poured Harvey in. This is your chance, Harvey, I
thought to myself. "C'mon, Harvey," I said out loud. He just lay
there at first, a little stunned, I guess. Then he perked up. He was
ready, I was sure, to begin some real exploring. But to my disappointment and amazement, *Harvey began to swim in a circle about
ten inches across and an inch below the surface of the water, like
the hands of a clock—just like in his bowl!*
    Years later the story became a metaphor. I realized that Howard,
Harvey, and too many people I have encountered over the last half
century swim in the same familiar, habitual circles, even when
reality changes, when opportunities to expand and explore appear,
or fresh needs and new resources emerge. As if thoroughly programmed or conditioned—psychologists call it "repetition compulsion," or more simply "neurosis"—we do the same old things over
and over again. This is tragically true of churches and church
leaders. Times change continuously and dramatically, but many
churches have not changed with the times.
    Viability and vitality in the local church depend on under-
standing, welcoming, and responding creatively to change. Static
leadership and unchanging organizational models will fail. The
church must embrace change, be it orderly or chaotic, because
without change there is no life, no passion, no commitment.
    Even to contemplate the work of rediscovery and reinvention
demands a substantial, even radical rethinking of basic, long-held,
apparently reliable assumptions. Nicodemus offers a case in point
(John 3:1-21). As the respected and learned rabbi approached Jesus
under the cover of night, he did not seem particularly lost or
confused. A teacher of the law, he thought and taught from an
ordered and confident worldview. Everything seemed in its place,
yet somehow he had come up a few pieces short. Maybe this
itinerant rabbi could help. After a strange and apparently brief
conversation, Nicodemus walked away, sorry, I would guess, that
he had asked. He seemed bewildered and confused, but so do I when
I ponder Jesus' answers to his rather straightforward questions.
    When you need gasoline for the mower, you arrive at the
service station with a five-gallon can. When you walk to a neigh-
bor's to borrow some sugar, you knock with a cup in your hand. So
when Nicodemus confronted Jesus that night, he arrived with an

"answer-shaped container" to carry home Jesus' reply. He may
have expected new thoughts—but Jesus spoke instead of a new
way of thinking. It is unsettling, even downright threatening, to
loosen our grip on comfortable and familiar ways of thinking. But
it must be done.

## Glue and Solvent

Two intricate and complex treatment strategies from psycho-
therapeutic process carry unexpected and colloquial names—
"glue" and "solvent." A *glue* approach is appropriate when a
patient's life is in significant disarray, ego structure is in some stage
of disintegration, and life is coming apart. The therapist works with
the patient to reassemble, reintegrate, bring back together what is
fracturing, to "glue" the person and his or her personality back into
place. Conversely, the *solvent* approach is timely when the ego
structure is in an exaggerated state of rigidity, when functioning is
wooden and unduly predictable, when life is too tightly held together. The therapist works to allow, even encourage, disintegration, to let things unravel and come apart, to let "solvent" dissolve
the basic configuration of the personality.

When a glue approach will work, we by all means use it. Often,
however, a solvent is required. This strategy can be troubling and
disorienting. It usually requires an extended period of transition; it
demands courage in the face of unavoidable anxiety and fear. It involves
grieving, letting go, and trusting. The new self emerges slowly and
remains a mystery for a time. I am convinced that reinventing the
congregation may demand just such a time-consuming, risky, and
thoroughgoing process of radical change. Rigid and predictable,
the church may need a hearty dose of solvent.

Someone said it well: We do not think our way to a new way of
living, but rather live our way to a new way of thinking. Such
learning entails solvent, changes in

• *perception:* We alter our perspective, looking through fresh and
clearer lenses, moving beyond perceptual selectivity to a more
comprehensive and objective view of the world.

• *internal processing:* Child psychologists believe that children
at age six begin to form a worldview that tends to become final by
ages twelve to fifteen. Endless additional facts may be added across

a lifetime, but the way they are stored and processed may continue to provide relatively static mental models and cognitive maps. Much adult behavior results from largely unthinking stimulus-response transactions.

• *range of options:* Laboratory researchers make a troubling observation: Rats fathom a maze faster than humans. Even more troubling is a specific detail of their findings—that only humans will repeat, again and again, a dead-end path. True learning expands the spectrum of behavioral options. Broadened perception and creative thinking produce previously unimagined options. There are more choices and a greater capacity for truly choosing.

• *the courage to act:* Psychotherapists are constantly baffled by patients' ability to look more deeply at their lives, envision new options rich in possibility, only to remain immobilized to step forward and act on their insight. Endless planning processes in local churches have produced stirring vision and creative plans but little action. True learners tolerate the inevitable risk of breaking out of comfortable, familiar, but self-defeating and fruitless patterns.

## Crisis in Our Era

The Western world forms its written language by a succession of shapes we call letters, clustered to form words, then grouped to form sentences and paragraphs that are logical and orderly. The Chinese form written language through a system of shapes that form pictures. Though these picture words are written vertically in an orderly way, this language is more holistic, as if this language "speaks," even as it writes. The language "draws" its meaning. The Chinese character for *crisis* is a fascinating case in point. It is formed, in fact, by combining two other characters—one for *danger*, the other for *opportunity*.

Crisis in our era is the child of change, not that change is new. Twenty-five hundred years ago Heraclitus said, "Nothing is permanent but change." Nuclear physicist Robert Oppenheimer wrote:

> One thing that is new is the prevalence of newness, the changing scale and scope of change itself, so that the world alters as we walk in it, so that the years of a person's life measure not some small growth, or rearrangement, or moderation of what was learned in childhood, but a great upheaval. What is new is that in one generation our knowledge of the

natural world engulfs, upsets, and supplants all knowledge of the natural world before.[4]

As much as we might yearn for glue in our life, it appears that solvents occur more naturally. Scientists have learned more about nature in my lifetime than was learned in the five thousand years before I was born. Ninety percent of the scientists who have ever lived are alive now. If you read the *New York Times* last week, you were exposed to more information in that one edition than the average person in colonial America was exposed to in a lifetime.

I sat with a group not long ago on a remote beach along the eastern Long Island coast, and our older son direct-dialed his brother in an even more remote village in central Mexico. Insisting it could not be done, even as I punched out the numbers, I direct-dialed a colleague who was working for the summer as a volunteer with the late Mother Teresa's Sisters of Charity on the streets of Calcutta, India. Two rings and he answered!

Lights in a home can turn on and off at a voice command, and voice-activated computers will transcribe verbal dictation then spell-check for accuracy. I was startled, and not a little troubled, to read that thoughts from our brains emit a detectible and trackable electronic signal that computers may soon be trained to receive and record. I can plant a tape recorder to capture what you say, but soon a hidden computer may eavesdrop on your thoughts!

There are more Muslims than Methodists and more Hindus than Presbyterians in Chicago. There are 123 nationalities in the Dade County, Florida, school system. By the turn of the century 57 percent of the work force will be minorities, and by the time my sons retire, Caucasians will be the minority in the United States. In 1950 the global population was 2.5 billion; it is projected to be 6.5 billion by the year 2000.

This accelerating change means more and more information is available, and thus the demand for larger and more agile retrievers and containers is increasing. But at some point, like bursting wineskins, the ways we organize and structure knowledge itself must change. It is a time of crisis, of danger and opportunity.

## The Arrival of New Dimensions

A transition from one era to the next is usually perceived only in retrospect. The era may go unnamed for decades. One can argue that the industrial age began in the mid-1700s, but it did not bear that name until Arnold Toynbee used it in 1940. Some suggest that the modern era, that sweep of history from which we are emerging, began with the Copernican revolution five hundred years ago. This so-called modern era oriented and stabilized its inhabitants, built as it was on the reliability of Newtonian physics, the ideal of scientific objectivity, the security of relatively stable nation-states, the acceptance of regional domains, the bridle of civility, and the acceptance, at times reluctantly, of a ruling class. But now this paradigm of global order is fracturing.

Rationalism, with its emphasis on objectivity and scientific method, first loosened the grip of the Judeo-Christian worldview three hundred years ago, but that worldview had significantly shaped the search for meaning in the Western world for eighteen hundred years. And one cannot study the Western world without exploring the sometimes nonrational interface of theological thought and ecclesiastical institutions and political, economic, and social history. Now, however, in decline for three hundred years, the Judeo-Christian story at the root of much of that theological and ecclesiastical world—its ethical mandates, spiritual practice, and political and social prerogatives—has clearly and precipitously fallen from relevance.

There may be moments in history when the coming of a new age can be noted even as it is beginning. I believe we are witnessing such a moment. This newly emerging era may elude easy naming, refusing to coalesce in any clear or consistent way, but a new day is dawning. Transition itself may become a semipermanent state of affairs. Emergence may be a fact of life.

Yet some among us seem either unwilling or incapable of imagining new possibilities for understanding and interpreting the world. Edwin Abbot's novella *Flatland* provides a powerful illustration of our current state of affairs.[5] The main characters are rectangles, lines, squares, and other two-dimensional geometrical forms.

One of the characters, Square, has a dream in which it is transported to a place where inhabitants live in only one dimension.

They are all lines. Square's efforts to share with them the news of a second dimension are met with skepticism and hostility.

After Square awakes from his dream, he encounters a character who lives in three dimensions: a sphere. But sadly, his attempts to share with fellow Flatlanders the news of a third dimension are soundly rejected. He becomes an outcast. He expresses in his memoirs, written from prison, his hope that his words will one day be read by an understanding mind.

Paradigm shift is no less dramatic. Old assumptions, cherished as reliable and somehow ultimately and eternally true, suddenly fall into disarray. This is a time of crisis, of danger and opportunity. Too many churches live in one dimension, let alone two, instead of three. George Barna, who has compiled extensive demographic data and tracked both sweeping and subtle contemporary social change, speaks an unsettling and challenging word to the church. Society, Barna suggests, changes dramatically every three to five years. The local church, he observes, changes every twenty-five to forty years![6]

## Warning Cries

When I reflect on the current state of the church, an image of an ill-fated parade comes to mind. Imagine you are part of that parade. Toddlers are perched on their fathers' shoulders, helium balloons dancing from strings tied to their wrists. Teenagers in baggy jeans and oversized tee shirts, their faces brightly painted with the colors of their high school teams, whirl and dance and high-five along the curb. The thunder of the bass drums sounds a cadence. Newcomers pour in from doorways and side streets, and the crowd swells.

The parade route, you assume, has been carefully mapped. Barricades block the side streets to point the way, and a police motorcycle brigade leads the line of march. Echoes of the brass band reverberate, and the tone is exuberant. People lean from open windows, and children wave flags along the curb. Everyone loves a parade!

You stand on your toes, then jump up and down, to catch a glimpse ahead. The parade is headed toward a gaping chasm from a massive excavation in the middle of the street! You see huge cranes twisting and straining, their buckets dropping rocks and

earth into waiting dump trucks. The bucket of a crane falls deep
into the opening before it hauls up its next load. "We'll turn at the
next intersection," you comfort yourself. The throng surges straight
ahead. "The grand marshal has surely noticed," you mutter silently,
but he is too busy waving this way and that. "The motorcycle
brigade will halt the march," you assure yourself. But they are too
engaged in their precision maneuvers and absorbed by the acclaim
of the crowd.

You cry out a warning, but your voice is absorbed in the mount-
ing din, and your gestures go unnoticed. You dig in your heels, but
momentum carries you and the throng, uninterrupted, straight
ahead. Those who do hear you only scoff. You cannot even slow
the pace. You try to wedge your way out, first to the left, then to the
right, but you are locked in. The march moves inexorably forward!

The dilemma of the church may be unfolding far less dramatically. Rather than marching toward a cliff, the church may be
stumbling into a fog bank, wandering and meandering more than
marching. The church may be exiting with more whimper than
bang, its story more comic than tragic. The church, in the eyes of
those beyond its doors, may be limping toward a death of irrele-
vance: Few care; fewer yet notice.

Many warning cries to local churches are as effective as the
unheard or unheeded cries from the parade. Pastors and lay leaders
seem more depressed than anguished. I hear not cries of pain but
the inaudible moans of the psychically numbed. Church officers tell
me that they drive home from too many meetings drained, frustrated, and angry, haunted by the gnawing question, What difference does it make anyway? A pastoral colleague, looking
demoralized and discouraged, muttered to me over breakfast, "I
seriously wonder whether it makes any difference at all that I got
up this morning, went to the office, worked on another sermon,
scheduled another pastoral visit, or did any of those things on my
list for today."

In the face of this reality I want to be pastoral and sensitive to
both the discouragement and the discouraged, but I want to be
forthright and candid as well. I believe that individual Christians,
their churches, and their leaders need a brisk wake-up call. Casual
interest or mere curiosity will not be enough. We must discern the

full magnitude of the moment. We must hear and then heed the voice
of the prophet in this time of crisis, of danger and opportunity.

## Old Testament Wisdom

Some of the Old Testament prophets, such as Amos, Micah, and
Isaiah thundered in from the countryside, shouted their tumultuous
message, then left. Others, such as Hosea, Nathan, Ezekiel, and
Jeremiah, lived in the neighborhood. Townspeople saw them at
their front doors, passed them on the village streets, and met them
at the market. These prophets spoke their message as they lived
among their countrypeople. I find Jeremiah's message in particular
to be most compelling.

### The Lord's Song in a Strange Land

In the years preceding the fall of Jerusalem, two prophets vied
for the ears and hearts of the people. Jeremiah insisted that a crisis
was at hand. Hananiah scoffed that Jeremiah was an alarmist.
Jeremiah, confiding that he wished Hananiah was right, finally
said, "Listen, Hananiah, the LORD has not sent you, and you have
made this people trust in a lie" (Jeremiah 28:15, RSV). Jeremiah
accused the priests and false prophets, among them Hananiah, of
"healing the wound lightly" (Jeremiah 6:14; 8:11), a most provocative metaphor. Hananiah counseled a bandage; Jeremiah, surgery. Hananiah focused on symptoms; Jeremiah saw disease.
Hananiah prevailed. He captured the attention and won the following of the people. In 586 B.C., however, the unthinkable happened:
Jerusalem fell to the Babylonians and the temple was destroyed.

Before the final siege, Jeremiah led a first contingent into captivity, but only after he purchased a field in Jerusalem, a symbol of
his confidence that the people would one day return. He led them
into a foreign land where it would be difficult to sing the Lord's
song, but he knew that defeat, though an ending, was also a
beginning.

Efforts by the contemporary church to "heal the wound lightly"
appear tempting. Hananiah's voice is appealing. We hear it everywhere, including within ourselves. "If only we do this or that, all
will be well." First aid will do. Simply prescribe the right medication and keep on marching.

We need, instead, Jeremiah's courage and wisdom. The road toward a reinvented church may lead through a season of captivity, a wilderness sojourn, a time of "singing the Lord's song in a strange land." No less a challenge and call needs to be urgently sounded. Transformation demands that certain things die and a time of chaos be endured before new life can emerge. Transformation of the church in our generation may mean living through a time not unlike that of Jeremiah and his generation.

### From Curiosity to Readiness

A scriptural narrative five hundred years prior to Jeremiah makes a similar point in a different historical context. The most remembered and formative biblical story for Jews and Judaism is the Exodus story. Third-world Christians find this a powerful and renewing story for the present era. First-world Christians may need to listen as well to a fresh hearing of its message and meaning.

After 480 years of captivity in Egypt, the children of Israel cried out and the Lord heard their cry. The liberation narrative begins with that deep and relentless cry and unfolds in earnest when a wandering shepherd approaches a bush burning in the desert. The sequence of events in that crucial moment deserves a closer look (Exodus 3). The Lord signaled a readiness and desire to be present to Moses—in a flame that burned but did not consume, and through the voice of an angel. Now it was not uncommon for a bush to burn in the desert. By a kind of spontaneous combustion, a lonely bush could leap, inexplicably, into flame. Moses, alert and watchful, willing and ready to respond, noticed. Though it appeared he mustered little more than simple curiosity, he walked closer. Then, as if responding to Moses' responsiveness, the Lord spoke, "Moses, Moses."

"Here I am," Moses answered. The delicate dialogue continued.

The voice instructed Moses to take off his shoes, for "the place on which you are standing is holy ground." God then spoke in the fullness of divine presence and the awesomeness of divine power. Moses trembled, covering his face, afraid. He tried to backpedal, venturing excuses, deflecting the divine mandate. He argued that he did not know God's name, trying to shun this mantle of leadership. "I AM WHO I AM," God answered. "Tell them, 'I AM has sent me to you.'"

"I am a stutterer and stammerer," Moses pleaded. "Find someone else."

"I will send Aaron as your companion," God countered.

"I have no power," Moses cried in desperation.

"What's in your hand?" God asked.

What he held in his hand had become so familiar, so much a part of his very person, Moses had to look at his hand to see. "My shepherd's staff," he muttered.

God instructed him to throw it on the ground, and when he did, it became a serpent. God told him to pick it up, and once again it became his staff. Finally, weary of Moses' resistance, God thundered, "Moses, go!" And he did.

The heart of Pharaoh hardened, and the will of the Hebrews faltered. But a promise was captured in a simple phrase: "a land flowing with milk and honey." And a destination beckoned: the Promised Land. Scenes of beauty and bounty became etched on their minds, clear and compelling, empowering confidence and commitment. The days and nights of liberation were demanding and frightening. The journey to freedom was long and arduous. A two-week walk from the Red Sea shore to the Jordan crossing took forty years!

The journey of faithfulness toward reinventing the church may unfold like the Exodus story, and a leader like Moses may illumine a pathway for that journey. Envision no less dramatic a call, no less emboldened a leadership, no less compelling a vision, no less determined a people. Be challenged to discern the presence of God in the midst of the ordinary. Let curiosity enlarge into readiness. Take off your shoes when you sense you are on holy ground. Be ready to tremble before the very presence of God. Name your hesitations and honor your resistances. Discover God's name anew. Find companions of varying gifts for the journey. Discover and claim the sources of power that may be near at hand. Focus a vision clear enough to yield metaphors that inspire and empower. Be patient and resilient, ready to take years to complete what, it would seem, could be accomplished in weeks. The fully reinvented church may come into its fullness well beyond our personal span of years. And it may look like nothing we would recognize from our present vantage point.

## Telling the Truth

In Scripture, stories of transformation are journey stories. Typically, these narratives consume more time than their characters expect, and they demand more of them than they ever anticipated. Abraham left Ur of Chaldees with no idea that before God's promise would be fulfilled, twenty-five years would pass. Jacob dreamed, as he rested his head on a stone pillow at Bethel, with no idea that his sojourn would wend through a decade and more. If they had known they would wander for forty years in the wilderness, the children of Israel might have remained forever in the grip of Egyptian slavery. As his personal reflections reveal in Galatians and as Luke reports in Acts, Paul spent three years in Arabia "recovering" from his conversion experience and as many as nine years in a ministry of minimal success before his missionary work bore fruit.

Those who dare to lead at the cutting edge, who dare to blaze fresh trails toward the reinvented future church, need to muster this kind of determination and stamina. I am convinced that those who will give leadership to a renewed and renewing church are those who will dare to experience both pain and possibility, then challenge the church to risk the same. This is a time of crisis, of danger and opportunity.

## Green Leaves and Death

I find an incident from the last week of Jesus' life perplexing and troubling. As Mark tells it, it was Monday after Palm Sunday as Jesus and the disciples returned to Bethany. Hungry, Jesus approached a fig tree covered with leaves, found no figs to eat, and cursed the tree. Tuesday morning they were walking the same path and came upon that same tree, dead to its roots.

"What does that story mean?" a woman in a Bible study group once asked me. Stalling for time and hesitant to admit how confounded I also was by this incident, I relied on the old "some scholars say" approach. "Some wonder if he was angry, frustrated at the thickheadedness of his disciples," I offered. "Others suggest this was a sign of the swiftness with which death would come upon him," I continued. "Still others focus on Jesus' long discourse following the story with its emphasis on the power of prayer," I concluded, knowing that none of these interpretations worked, really, not even for me.

One long-time member of that group, Sara, was a horticulturist by profession, and her reflections were often fresh and insightful. I remember how her eyes lit up that day as she offered her interpretation of the story, one that still makes the most sense of any to me. "There are certain plants and trees, fig trees among them," she explained, "that the season before they die sprout leaves fuller and greener than ever before." In effect, the tree has already died. This last springtime of full, lush, green leaves is a grand deception. To a discerning eye the fact is clear. This tree is dead. "I wonder," she mused, "if this fig tree isn't like the Pharisees—green and healthy looking on the outside but dead on the inside. Jesus didn't kill it. He just told the truth about it."

If this was meant as a wake-up call to institutional Judaism of Jesus' time, its leaders slept through it. I fear that in our time as well many so-called renewal strategies for local churches may only produce bright green shoots that mask ecclesiastical dying.

## Getting Lost

It is a not unfamiliar story. You are the driver. The car is full, and you are headed off to a meeting several towns away. You are off the main road, and you have made a wrong turn, but no one has noticed. You are too stubborn to stop and check the map or ask for directions, so you just keep driving. Your sense of direction lets you down, every attempt to find your way back fails, and you completely lose your bearings. Finally someone dares to ask, "Are we lost?"

"Yes," you answer sheepishly.

"How lost?"

"I have no idea!" you are forced to admit.

It is tempting to keep on driving—like Harvey swimming in that incessant circle. I'll lose five pounds, buy a new wardrobe, get a sportier car. I'll smoke a cigarette, splash on a sexier cologne, find a younger woman. I'll read the right book, go to the right seminar, find the right guru. We'll sing zippier hymns, get new choir robes, produce a snazzier newsletter. He's the wrong minister, we need new officers, I'll try another church.

"How lost are we?"

"I dunno."

As a consultant, I am often asked to provide congregational assessment. There are no diagnostic machines to hook up to a church, no blood tests or biopsies, no X rays or MRIs. But data can be collected and the system carefully observed and analyzed. There are symptoms to be noted and organizational dynamics to examine. I try to be as objective as possible, while being sensitive and thoughtful as well. Pastors and church officers would prefer medication to surgery, minor repairs to costly overhauls. I am no stranger to the temptation to speak a comforting and reassuring word when more troublesome feedback is called for. But someone has to tell the truth.

Moses had a vision of a promised land, but Dothan wanted to make do in bondage. "All's well," Hananiah assured the people. "Jeremiah is making trouble. We need make only minor adjustments." "I wish Hananiah was right," Jeremiah confessed, "but he's not." The Prodigal Son made the best of it for a while in a far country, but then "came to himself" and faced the truth about himself. Some chose, despite Paul's warning, to remain conformed to this world, refusing transforming renewal of their minds. Someone had to tell the truth.

I am convinced that too many churches are in denial, refusing to name their "bondage," their "healing of the wound lightly," their "far country." Courageously naming this reality, a prophetic task, as unsettling as it inevitably will be, can begin the journey back to faithfulness. But my assessment is not as important as yours. What is your far country as an individual or a congregation? How far off course are you? How lost?

## The Courage to Leave

Biblical narratives remind us that transformation begins with courage to leave. Accounts of dramatic change in the lives of the people of God are told in the Bible in story form, usually journey stories. And those stories begin with leaving. Abram's arriving at Canaan had meant, twenty-five years earlier, leaving Ur of the Chaldees—a walled city, safe and familiar. To become the leader of Israel, Moses left the safety and anonymity of the plains of Moab. Crossing the Jordan into the Promised Land had meant, forty years before, leaving Egypt—captivity to be sure, but safety and predictability. Ur of the Chaldees, the plains of Moab, Egypt—each a symbol of safety and familiarity—are difficult to leave. The moment of letting go and leaving is both awesome and agonizing. Ask Abraham, Sarah, or Moses; ask Amos, Micah, or Jeremiah; ask Peter, Andrew, or James; ask Paul, Silas, or Barnabas.

We must be careful not to minimize or romanticize this leaving. People fall in love with the familiar. They cling to the safe and secure, even when it clearly does not work! And the same is true of congregations. Churches fall in love with their buildings, become attached to their familiar routines, and sanctify their traditions.

Recently I led a Recovering the Sacred Center workshop for seventeen church leaders, lay and clergy. Midway through the first session I asked a question I typically ask early on: What's working, and what's not working? I ask that question in an intentionally ambiguous way. What's working or not working for you personally? Professionally? As an individual, a member, or a leader in your church? As a committee, a task force, a board, or as a total congregation?

As is usually the case, this group responded with a broad variety of thoughts—reflections and insights, analysis and evaluation, theory and conjecture. And they offered just as broad a variety of feelings—joys and struggles, appreciations and resentments, hope and discouragement, delight and dismay.

Many books and articles, including several published in the past year, seek to chart directions, identify trends, and list reliable assumptions and conclusions about this paradigm-shifting time in which we are living, to fathom the new world that is unfolding before us. Responses from this workshop group seemed congruent with those of other groups, and also with what these books and articles have concluded:

- Church attendance and financial receipts are declining, and signs of any bottoming out seem hard to find.
- The typical response to people in authority is dramatically shifting.
- Lay leaders are harder to recruit, and many seem discouraged and burned out.
- Seminary training seems to have inadequately prepared ministers for the everyday demands and responsibilities of leadership, and lay leaders feel undertrained as well.

- Local churches seem organized for a social reality that no longer exists.
- Traditional program strategies are receiving diminishing response.
- Leaders, particularly the clergy but lay leaders as well, find their families increasingly resentful of the time and emotional energy they give to the church, and they find their own level of self-care inadequate.

As these church leaders at the workshop were sharing their thoughts and feelings, I drew a circle on a piece of newsprint to represent the church. Some of their issues and concerns seemed to reside within the church, so I recorded them inside the circle. Then I recorded those that focused on their private lives outside the circle. As the conversation subsided, I suggested we had two options. We could prioritize these items, then address each of them in turn, workshop-style, by planning a series of problem-solving sessions in search of creative responses to each issue. That might seem appealing, logical, and potentially fruitful.

But I advocated another approach. I invited them to set aside all these issues—those inside and those outside the church—at least initially. Name them as important—even pressing and urgent—but put them on hold. My invitation to you is to move in another, perhaps new and different direction. It may at first hearing make little sense to you. It is to recover the sacred center, to become quiet, to begin to journey inward, to seek a holy ground on which to stand. The response of a longtime and admittedly discouraged lay leader seemed to speak for the rest. "It doesn't make a whole lot of sense. I'm not sure I really understand. But something about it seems right. Let's do it." She had the courage to leave.

You, the readers of this book, are likely experiencing the same problems, frustrations, and concerns as those in the workshop. I offer the same invitation to you—to leave your safe place and to join an inward journey toward the sacred center as a starting place for renewal.

## Entering the Next Room

According to Swedish organizational psychologist Claes Janssen, each individual, group, organization, or congregation "lives" in a four-room apartment. Over time the action moves from one room to another. *Contentment* characterizes the room where most of us would prefer to stay. It is where we find stability and familiar routine. We know the rules and follow them, and the routine is predictable. The room feels safe and secure. Inevitably, things change, but we do not notice, or do not want to. So we enter *denial.* We pretend nothing has changed, that all is well, while we suppress our fear and anxiety. It is amazing how long we can stay there. We remain stuck until we own up to our feelings and wake up to reality, or someone or something wakes us up. Then we move on to *confusion,* where the fear and anxiety will be either crippling or life-giving. "Every new project, course correction, major change requires optimal anxiety," states Janssen. "If there's too much, we are paralyzed, too little, unmotivated." This is the most difficult, painful, and frightening room in the apartment, but it is the birth-place of renewal. If we rise to its challenge, it will yield its gifts, and we emerge into *renewal,* only, of course, to live this continual circular process again.

This book is a wake-up call in the midst of the church's denial, a challenge to enter courageously that place called confusion—with all its anxiety, chaos, turmoil, and uncertainty—that we might sound a word of hope that renewal awaits in the next room.

*Chapter Two*

# Recovering the Sacred Center
## In Search of a Definition

### I Tell You a Mystery

"I tell you a mystery," Paul concedes in the midst of twenty-three verses of gallant effort to explain a foundational Christian concept: the resurrection body (1 Corinthians 15:35-58). "Some will ask, 'How can the dead be raised to life? What kind of body will they have?'" He employs a fascinating and powerful array of metaphors and analogies, pressing the capacity of his language to its limits. He borrows a metaphor from nature: the wonder and mystery of a seed growing from tiny speck to full-grown tree, dying, he reminds the reader, before it bursts into life. He uses an analogy from Hebrew thought: the terrestrial must put on the celestial. He then taps the Greek worldview: the mortal must put on immortality. He launches a volley of taunting sarcasm lifted from Isaiah and Hosea: "Where, death, is your victory? Where, death, is your power to hurt?" (v. 55, GNB). He even quotes himself from an earlier letter: "We will be changed in an instant, in the blinking of an eye, with a trumpet blast!" But ultimately, after he has wrestled from language all it seems able to yield, he admits, "Lo, I tell you a mystery."

Jesus takes a similar approach when defining the kingdom of God. If a single theme stands at the center of all other themes in the teaching of Jesus, it is the kingdom of God (or the kingdom of heaven). Jesus was approached by people who longed to understand and experience this kingdom—Nicodemus under the cover of night, Zacchaeus perched in a tree, and blind Bartimaeus in a crowded village square, just to name a few. On other occasions Jesus initiated teaching on the theme—forty-four times in the Gospel of Matthew, eleven in the Sermon on the Mount alone. Inquirers wanted to understand this kingdom, and Jesus wanted to define it with compelling clarity. It is noteworthy, however, that Jesus at no point says, "The kingdom of God *is* . . . ," but always, "The kingdom of God is *like*. . . ." As vital as this theme is, it ultimately eludes clear definition. As much as Jesus yearns for every hearer to comprehend and enter that kingdom, there is no simple prescription or five-step program. Only, simply, "The kingdom of God is like. . . . "

We are familiar with the explanations Jesus or Paul used with some frequency to interpret the themes of the faith. Phrases like "born again" and "in Christ" come immediately to mind. But what is even more striking to me is how infrequently Jesus and Paul repeated themselves. Neither seemed to embark on a preaching, teaching, and healing mission armed with answers to the most frequently asked questions in hand. It must have been tempting for them to refine explanations to foundational concepts and then to offer them as predictable situations arose, but it appears they did not. Rather, they tuned to the unique reality of each moment, and the uniqueness of each person, and offered constantly new explanations.

So it is with the cornerstone concept of this chapter and of this book—recovering the sacred center. Just what is the sacred center? What does it mean to recover that sacred center? And, perhaps most important, how do we recover the sacred center? I will suggest that the sacred center—of a person and of a local church—is very real, to be taken very seriously, a source of personal and congregational transformation. I want this chapter, and those that follow, to make clear not only what the sacred center is, but how to experience it. I want to speak with clarity, precision, and persuasiveness. But inevitably, ultimately *I tell you a mystery: the sacred center is like....*

This is the case partly because the world of thought and the structure of language are in many ways dissonant by definition. Language is linear and sequential; words and sentences follow one another. Reality, on the other hand, and thinking about reality are a totality, an intricate system of interwoven and interrelated parts. Language is one- or two-dimensional, and reality is three-dimensional.

This chapter explores a concept—the sacred center—that eludes a concise definition. Yet it is that very totality that I want to share in a clear and compelling way. If it took six wise men of India to describe an elephant ("for all of them were blind"), recovering the sacred center may become clearer as we examine it from more than one vantage point. Any one view may have more meaning for one person and less for another. But taken together, I trust that they will deepen our shared understanding of this cornerstone concept.

## Your Heart Knows the Way

A generation ago my friend Raquel Peniazek was one of South America's finest concert performers, a pianist and singer. A native of Uruguay, she was brought to the United States by Rudolf Serkin of Curtis Institute in Philadelphia. As she became older, she gave up her concert work and became a master teacher. Singers, musicians, choral directors, dancers, and composers would come by the hundreds for her master's classes.

Raquel developed her own unique way of coaxing the highest and best from her students, at once musical and mystical. I watched her one day in her living room as she worked with a young tenor. "Technically, your singing is outstanding, even extraordinary," she said. "You are very gifted. But something, *something* is missing." She stood up, walked slowly toward him, then placed her hand on his chest. "Let me help you discover your song, the song of your heart," she said. "Hear it first. Then I'll help you sing it. But until you hear your song, don't sing."

I chatted one day with Raquel about preaching and leadership in the church. She placed her hand on my chest. It was warm and steady and strangely powerful. "Discover your song, Howard. Hear the song. Then sing it."

I am reminded of a story I heard about lyricist Oscar Hammerstein. Just before he died, he wrote a few last words that tell us "a song's not a song 'til you sing it" and "love isn't love 'til you give it away."

The sacred center is about the songs of our hearts to be given away, about hearing our song and then singing it. But in noisy, frantic, overbooked, and overextended lives, how do we even begin to hear our song? A brief incident from a two-hour meeting may suggest a response.

Some years ago I led a planning meeting for some leaders of Covenant Church. Though they brought a long-standing and persistent commitment to their church, they found the church's life and ministry increasingly distant from the demands and priorities of their everyday lives. They did not want this planning process to be what one elder called "more of the same." Though it was not what I had planned, I found myself beginning the session by telling them the story I once heard of a journalist who some years ago wrote an article in which her goal was to put her finger on the pulse of the American people.

This journalist decided to conduct hundreds of interviews all across the country—young and old, rich and poor, differing ethnic groups, as full a cross section as possible. She met them in shopping malls, along the streets of cities, towns and villages, in waiting rooms, wherever people were willing to give her half an hour or so. She asked them just three questions.

The first question was simply: "What do you want?" Typical respondents were quizzical and uncertain at first. But a momentum would quickly build, and they would often talk for eight or ten minutes. As that first response ebbed, she asked her second question: "What do you want?"

"You just asked that," was the predictable reply.

"I know," she would say, "but that is the second question too: What do you want?" The responder's resistance quickly gave way to a wave of fresh thoughts, often more poignant and intimate than the first, as people talked about a deeper layer of wanting. When this second response began to end, she asked the third question, which most people being interviewed anticipated.

"I know," they would say, "What do you want?" And they would commence to speak again, often more eagerly and at greater length, usually in even deeper and more heartfelt ways. They reported that her persistent, repeated question could have been asked again and again, and that each asking seemed to take them toward the center of themselves.

This journalist wrote her article, summarizing the similarities and differences she observed in the content of what people had said.

But what most struck her was a single comment made in one way or another by almost every person interviewed—that they were rarely asked, "What do you want?" by anyone, including, sadly, even those closest to them. And, they hastened to admit, they rarely asked themselves that question. And if they did, they did not even listen very well to themselves.

When I finished telling the story, I invited the Covenant Church leaders to ask themselves that question: What do you want? What do you long for? What do you yearn for? I asked them to reflect silently for ten minutes before sharing with the others. In the quietness, I felt a certain hesitation about asking such a personal question.

My concern was quickly dispelled. The group was immediately relaxed, trusting, and intimate. Those words—wanting, longing, yearning—had opened up something deep within them. When they had finished sharing, they decided this was exactly what they wanted their church to be—a place that invited people to be open about what they were really thinking and feeling, a place where they were listened to and respected. They added reluctantly that often their church had not been this kind of place. As leaders, they began to work toward changing that.

Parish ministry, as a quest for the sacred center, can be helpfully guided by a single word: *longing*. This is a word whose very sound somehow stirs a desire for that of which it speaks. The words *chocolate chip cookie,* for instance, awaken "cookie hunger" in any self-respecting chocoholic, splash a smile across the face, and send him or her racing to the kitchen with the hope of finding that very treat. The word *beach* may stir a longing to race across the sand, leap through the shallow waves, throw yourself with abandon over the first cresting wave, then be startled by the crisp chill of an early summer plunge.

So it is for me when I hear the word *longing*. The mere sound of this word stirs in me, perhaps also in you, that of which it speaks. I experience an emotional tone of many subtle textures—a touch of sadness, yet something exhilarating as well; a stilling, yet a certain stirring too; a calming, yet also a restlessness. Longing quiets and settles me, draws me back from what has been occupying me, draws me deeper into myself. At the same time longing inclines me outward, makes me lean forward, energizes and animates me.

Someone at a workshop pondering this dynamic of longing said, "Longing calls me to my heart, and my heart knows the way."

"It's as if the longing of my heart is a 'homing device,'" another added.

The word *yearning* seems to carry similar power. My wife, Betsy, leads workshops at Temenos, the retreat center where we live, called "Yearning for God." When she asks the circle of participants in a new group, "Why have you come?" two or three invariably answer, "It was the title." "That word *yearning*," they will say, "just seemed to do something to me. It awakened something."

We are living, I am convinced, in a time when people throughout our culture are experiencing a deep sense of longing or yearning. Some yearn for meaning and values; others, for purpose and direction; still others, for fresh hope and renewed vitality. Many long for personal integrity and authentic relationship. Some call it "hunger," "deep desire," "an inner quest." Some refer to a vague, gnawing, persistent sense of emptiness. St. Augustine called it "restlessness," ultimately for God. Joseph Campbell called it our "bliss."

And we are living, I am also convinced, in a time when both traditional and more contemporary answers are proving equally empty and unfulfilling. Achievement and success have their rewards, and there are pleasures that money can buy. Reason can fathom much in life, and relationships are important, of course. Philosophies and psychotherapies offer insight and direction, and religious institutions, including churches, promise helpful answers and spiritual and nourishment. Koheleth, the Preacher or Philosopher in Ecclesiastes, however, may speak for many in our culture: "Vanity of vanities. . . . All is vanity" (Ecclesiastes 1:2).

The poet Rainer Rilke suggests an alternative. He counseled a younger poet to leap less quickly to answers, to learn to love and embrace the questions first.[1] The quest for the sacred center may begin with patiently and persistently listening, just listening, to the longing and yearning.

## Journeying toward the Inner Self

For this reason I fall on my knees before God, from whom every family in heaven and on earth receives its true name. I ask God from the wealth of God's glory to give you power through the

Spirit to be strong in your inner selves, and I pray that Christ may make his home in your hearts through faith. I pray that you may have your roots and foundation in love, so that you, together with all God's people, may have the power to understand how broad and long, how high and deep, is Christ's love. Yes, may you come to know his love—although it can never be fully known—and so be completely filled with the very nature of God. (Ephesians 3:14-19, GNB, adapted)

Fifteen years ago a colleague used this passage from Ephesians at a staff meeting to introduce a time of silence, reflection, and sharing. She read it from the Good News Bible, not usually my translation of choice. I heard the verses with fresh ears and immediately felt something being touched deep within me.

Over the years I have invited hundreds of people in countless groups—clergy events and judicatory seminars, adult classes and church board workshops, seminary classes and silent retreats, and especially Recovering the Sacred Center workshops—to ponder two simple questions as a way to engage the text. The responses have on virtually every occasion been remarkable and moving. I invite you to take a few moments to ponder these questions before you read the next few paragraphs, which describe how I use these verses and share the typical responses from these groups. I invite you also to use this exercise with groups you might lead.

I typically introduce the passage by noting several provocative words—"inner self," "true name," "home," and "heart." Then I ask participants to focus on the words "inner self." I write the two questions on newsprint, reading them aloud with brief additional interpretation.

1. *Who or what is your "inner self"?* What is Paul referring to? What other phrases might he have used? What other names might you use? In what ways is this inner self a different self from your everyday self? What qualities characterize this inner self?
2. *How do you connect to your inner self?* It appears that Paul wants you to connect to your inner self. How do you connect to it? How difficult do you find that connecting? How frequently do you do so? I invite participants to reflect on these questions as I read the text twice, indicating that we will have time for quiet individual reflection after the reading, to be followed by sharing in groups of three, then in the total group.

Most people become aware immediately that these questions are stirring something deep within them. They are often touched by the depth of sharing that ensues around the smaller, then larger circles. Common comments include the following: "My inner self is my 'higher self,'" "the self that God had in mind when God created me," "my heart, my essence, my very center," "the me that knows I am unconditionally loved and accepted by God," "the one in me who knows God, who is at one with God," "the real me." Typically, delightful variety yet intrinsic congruence mark the various responses.

"How quickly and easily I lose connection with my inner self," someone once confessed. "Sometimes it's a long road back," added another. "I'm not sure I've connected with my inner self in years," still another lamented. Others have revealed: "The journey to my inner self is my journey to God." "When I connect with my inner self I am able to truly pray." "My life is richer, my decisions are clearer, my relationships are more loving, life is more beautiful when I am close to my inner self." "My inner self is my true Teacher." "It knows the way, the truth, and the life." "I am more fully 'on track,' more confident and more effective, more faithful when I listen to my inner self." There are often nods around the circle as the collage of responses grows.

A business executive in his mid-forties, a newcomer, he said, to this kind of introspective experience, risked a fascinating reflection. "Look, it took a lot of time, effort, and creative energy to hone and perfect my personality. But sometimes I feel like a character in a play. I am playwright, director, and stage manager, as well as lead actor in my play. I'm an actor I send out into the world as a substitute for the real me. 'In today's performance the part of me is being played by Harold Dixon,' a voice announces as the day begins. I've created an appealing character, who speaks appealing lines, who does appealing things. People like him. They applaud him. And that's the tragedy. I don't want to become a better actor. I want to become me!"

I sometimes ask whether the sharing brings any passages of scripture to mind. "Our true identity is hidden with God in Christ," a retired food service executive offered. "When you are in Christ you are a new creation. Behold the old has passed away and the new has come," a high school student remembered.

A conviction seems to form around the average group that individual renewal as Christians and the transformation of churches call for a journeying toward the inner self, that place within where we come to know who we are and then what we are to do—both individually and collectively.

I can offer no clearer, more focused, more compelling definition of "the sacred center" than these paragraphs, which include the reflections of many people in many settings over more than a decade.

## Finding the Sacred Center

There is a persistent paradox woven through the journey motif in every culture's mythic quest stories: the Gilgamesh epic, history's oldest surviving work of fiction; *The Wandering Jew* and *Siddhartha, Don Quixote* and *The Canterbury Tales; Pilgrim's Progress* and *Paradise Lost;* the I Ching and the Bhagavad Gita. It is the ironic paradox of traveling outward in order to journey inward. The quest that traverses sea and mountain, that encounters danger and discouragement, is yet a movement downward and inward at the same time. "Out there" and "in here" are intimately connected. T. S. Eliot writes:

> We shall not cease from exploration
> And the end of all our exploring
> Will be to arrive where we started
> And know the place for the first time.[2]

This paradox is everywhere evident in the faith journeys I have been privileged to witness or accompany. The norm, the more common movement, perhaps, is to find the sacred center and then to move outward from it in love and service: inward journey, then outward journey, a sequence and rhythm. But just as often people find the sacred center as they live and serve: outward journey, then inward journey.

Bill had been a member of Gladwyne Church for eleven years, though he was always quick to say, "Mary joined, and we like to do things together, so I joined too, but this 'church thing' just doesn't make much sense to me, really." He worshiped infrequently and found church "meaningless and boring, if you want to know the truth." Christian teachings appeared confusing, mostly irrelevant to him. "Maybe there's a God, and maybe not. Who knows?" he once said with little expression in his voice. So I was surprised, and so was he, when he signed up for a ten-day mission trip to Haiti.

Bill joined a group of four headed to a community called San Fils on the edge of Port au Prince, the location of the "Home for the Destitute and Dying." His face betrayed an awkwardness and anxiety that we each felt, but the gentle manner of the sister who greeted us put him at ease. She handed Bill a container of skin cream and led him by the hand to a large room with twenty to twenty-five beds of tuberculosis patients. "Let someone catch your attention. You'll have plenty of choices," she instructed. "Go to his cot and rub cream into his skin, which you'll find dry and cracked from this low-humidity heat." An old man along the back wall caught his eye.

As Bill removed the cap from the container, the old man took off his pajama top, pulled up the bottoms to his thighs, tucked his arms under his pillow, and lay back with a warm smile. "I cannot ever remember feeling so uncomfortable," Bill confessed in our circle that evening. "It felt so overwhelmingly intimate. And I didn't even know his name!" Bill noticed immediately that the old man began to fix his eyes on him. Not a stare. More than mere curiosity. Simply a steady, quiet, rather lovely gaze. Bill could manage no more than fleeting, hesitant glances in response.

Hoping it might quiet his discomfort, Bill began to sing, though barely above a whisper at first. "Jesus loves me, this I know," he sang as he rubbed a first palmful of cream onto the man's hand and forearm. "For the Bible tells me so," he continued, as he pushed the cream up the old man's arm. One arm, then the other, left leg then right, singing this familiar children's song over and over again. As he began to massage cream into his chest, he felt a vibration. The old man was humming, line for line. Then he began to sing the words. The first line, then the second, until Bill and his new friend found themselves singing the whole song, in English, rather robustly. Broad smiles splashed across Bill's very white face and the old man's blue-black Haitian face, and tears rolled down each of their cheeks.

Their eyes met in a loving gaze, unselfconscious now, unhesitant and unbroken. "My heart simply broke open," Bill reported that evening, with a steadier eye contact around our circle than I had ever experienced from him before. "Some deep place in me came alive. I don't know what to call it. I felt so peaceful. So connected. To him, and to myself. And, yes, to God, I think."

Others tell stories of similar journeys. Tim had served the last platter from the back of the church van that was providing meals to a gathering of homeless people. He sat on a vent to talk to Donald, a regular at this corner, as they both munched hamburger casserole and green beans from paper plates. Suddenly Donald began to tremble, then break into a full-blown seizure. Tim cradled Donald's head to keep him from pounding himself into the metal grate and flexed his strong carpenter's arms to protect Donald until the convulsions subsided. "I've been a lifelong Christian," Tim shared in the van as they drove home, "but God has never touched me as deeply as tonight on that vent."

Susie had two daughters in private school and lived in a gracious suburban home. She heard about a team of people from her church who went weekly to visit an AIDS hospice in West Philadelphia. To her surprise, she signed up and soon became a regular. Her special buddy was Henry. Henry loved carrot cake and walnut brownies, which she brought with her on alternate weeks. The Sunday after Henry died, Susie wore his baseball cap to church and read the New Testament lesson. Those familiar words from Matthew, "just as you did it to one of the least of these" (25:4), spoke with fresh impact as she read them in her cracking, tear-punctuated voice. "I've been going to church since before I can remember, and I've always known myself as a Christian, but God found me, and I found myself when I found Henry. He opened his heart to me, and my heart opened," she later told me.

The sacred center is often found in the contemplative silence of inward journeying. But it is also discovered "out there" in the world. "Follow me," Jesus said over and over again, and those who responded found themselves and their God "on the way." "You are the Christ, the Son of the living God," exclaimed Peter, perhaps as far away from home as he had ever traveled (Matthew 16:16, RSV). "My Lord and my God," blurted Thomas, a country boy in the heart of a city (John 20:28). "Jesus, Son of David, have mercy on me," a blind beggar shouted in a teeming village square (Mark 10:47). "Today salvation has come to this house," a tax collector perched in a tree heard Jesus say as their eyes met (Luke 19:9).

I have been privileged to hear or witness many similar stories over the years. The sacred center is found in reeking slums and along trash-strewn city streets, in old-age homes and children's wards, in mental hospitals and AIDS hospices. It is found wherever human encounter, deepened by compassion and an open heart, opens to the sacred center. In Morris West's novel *Shoes of the Fisherman,* Kiril, the central character, says that we will hear in our voices as we minister to such as these, "a whisper of the voice of God."[3]

## Mystics, Contemplatives, and the Sacred Center

When I first encountered the writings of the Christian mystics, I felt like I was opening a door to a secret room full of treasures. This way of framing the Christian life felt wonderfully rich and exhilarating. Some call it contemplative theology. I think of it as home. And I have noticed the theme of recovering the sacred center woven clearly and boldly through the thousands of pages I have read. But I have been influenced particularly by two mystics—both sixteenth-century Spanish monks, each a central figure in reforming the Carmelite religious life—and by a contemplative monk of our century.

### Teresa of Avila

Teresa of Avila told her biographer that on the eve of Trinity Sunday, 1577, God showed her in a flash a whole book. In her vision, she reported seeing

a most beautiful crystal globe like a castle in which I saw seven dwelling places, and in the seventh, which was in the center, the King of Glory dwelt in the greatest splendor. From there He beautified and illumined all those dwelling places to the outer wall. The inhabitants received more light the nearer they were to the center.[4]

Teresa envisions the path of faithfulness as a journeying inward and downward through a series of "dwelling places" leading ultimately toward the seventh, the place of union with the divine, the sacred center. The outer walls of the castle, majestic and magnificent, represent in Teresa's imagery the body, looking primarily outward, lured by the appeals of the world away from the inner brilliance.

The first three dwelling places are reached by a combination of human effort and "ordinary grace." Spiritual curiosity, the first stirrings of spiritual desire, and prayer—though still hesitant, unpracticed, and undisciplined—lead the journeyer into the first chamber. Then, as receptivity deepens, new levels of determination mount, and "consolations" (Teresa's word for the rewards and satisfactions that accompany early spiritual exploration) are received, the pilgrim passes to the second dwelling place. Attachments to the world linger and commitment remains uneven, but perseverance, an essential quality for Teresa, rises to meet inevitable spiritual struggles. A spiritual longing purifies, a compassionate heart awakens, and the third dwelling place is entered.

The passage to the fourth chamber is of a different order—more supernatural, mystical, and contemplative. Teresa uses the image of a cistern. A cistern can be filled by an intricate system of aqueducts, designed and built by human ingenuity, or deep inner springs can bubble up. Aqueducts have filled the cistern in the first three chambers, but now those inner springs must be tapped. In the fifth chamber there is a first faint awareness of possibility for union with God, and Teresa employs a second analogy, a silkworm. She visions God as the cocoon in which the silkworm dies (the "old self" of Pauline writing), then emerges as a beautiful white butterfly. This inward, downward journey becomes paschal mystery, dying and rising with and in Christ. She uses courtship as a third analogy: The pilgrim is prepared as bride for bridegroom in readiness for the divine marriage.

Teresa writes most extensively of the sixth chamber, where courage and determination merge with supernatural grace and yield revelations, mysteries, visions, and ecstasies that lead the faithful one to a locked door that leads to the dwelling place of the King of Glory and the longed-for unitive experience. Teresa uses a final analogy, from the conversion of Paul. In the sixth room we are blinded by the immense light of the divine presence, as Paul was on the Damascus Road. In the seventh dwelling place, the scales fall from our eyes and we know the divine face to face, in ultimate communion, in utter illumination. What we had seen only through a glass darkly we now know fully.

Though journeying to this deepest inner chamber is a lifelong quest, there is daily invitation to revisit it in prayer and then to share its illumination.[5]

## St. John of the Cross

John of the Cross, though raised in the humble household of a sixteenth-century weaver and no stranger to poverty, gained admission to a Jesuit college and entered a Carmelite monastery at age twenty. Bright, strong-willed, rebellious in spirit, and a natural reformer, his was a turbulent monastic career, and the bitter resistance of his confreres landed him more than once in the monastery jail. In August 1578, having been locked in a windowless six-by-six-foot cell, suffocating in summer and bitterly cold in winter, and having been intermittently beaten for refusal to renounce his reforms, he escaped. Rather than become embittered, his thinking sharpened, his compassion for the poor deepened, his love of nature broadened, and the insights that were to become his major contributions became firm.[6]

His major works, companion pieces, are *Ascent of Mount Carmel* and *Dark Night of the Soul.* Where Teresa used descent to image the spiritual journey, John used ascent imagery. The high state of perfection, union with God through love, is a summit. This ascent is arduous, demanding high determination, stamina, and patience. And it demands a passage through an awesome, even terrifying "dark night." As in Teresa's cocoon, where death emerges into new life, one must "die with Christ."

John names three elements to this dark night. First, this is a dark night of *relinquishment*, detachment, and purification. All attachments and compulsions, unbridled desires, habitual inclinations, and undue affections must be pruned away. This means not merely negative attachments, but anything—person, idea, practice, or desire, even the apparently positive—that captivates our attention, will, and spirit. The greater the attachment, the greater the pain. Second, it is a dark night of *faith*, because we can walk only by faith, not sight. The gifts of reason and logic are affirmed but fall short of the full ascent of Mount Carmel. And third, it is a dark night of *God's communion with the soul*, because this grace is possible only with utter and total relinquishment of all intent and effort. This is a path of surrender. Then, beyond dark night, at the summit of the ascent, lies mystical union with Christ.

Common themes run through these and other mystical writings: (1) The sacred center, be it a chamber in the heart of a castle or the summit of a high and holy mountain, is very real. (2) Yet it is mysterious, mystical, and elusive, able to be explained only indirectly in poetry and metaphor. (3) The quest takes us inevitably, it seems, on a spiritual pilgrimage, a long and arduous journey to far and distant places. (4) Yet it is at the same time a journey inward and downward into our deepest self. (5) To venture this journey demands intent and tireless effort. (6) And yet that effort must at the right moment yield to grace alone.

### Thomas Merton

The contemplative who has spoken most poignantly and powerfully to me is a modern mystic, Thomas Merton. Sister Sharon Doyle, a monk from Nova Nada, a small community of monks in western Nova Scotia, teaches about a threefold journey to renewal suggested by Thomas Merton.

When Sharon leads retreats on Merton's thought, she sometimes makes use of a series of diagrams to guide the way. She begins with a circle, a line and arrow, and a second circle.

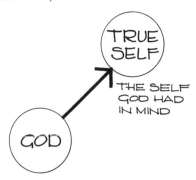

In the circle she writes GOD in bold letters. For the mystics, she explains, God has two distinct dimensions: transcendent God—creator, wholly other, ultimate mystery, and imminent God—close as breath, wholly one, infilling the everyday and ordinary. Bonhoeffer once referred to God as "the beyond in our midst." This God, awesome and omnipresent, is a creator God: "In [Christ] all things

in heaven and on earth were created … whether thrones or dominions or rulers or powers" (Colossians 1:15). The creation emanates
from and gives expression to the essence of the divine. THE SELF
GOD HAD IN MIND, she writes along the line emanating from
that center. Oak seeds grow into oak trees, robins' eggs hatch robins,
and bulbs grow faithfully and inevitably toward the spring flowers
they are encoded to become. But people and institutions are different. Each is invited and gifted to be a unique and precious human
being or institution. But unlike the plant and animal world, we
participate in our unfolding and becoming. We make choices. We
say yes or no. We may grow faithfully, but we do not grow
inevitably, toward what God intended us to be. Finally, she writes
TRUE SELF in the circle at the point of the arrow. God longs to
give unique self-expression in every person and congregation.

After a time for solitude, silence, and reflection, Sharon uses a
second diagram to lead seekers into the next phase of their journey.
She draws a second line, arrow, and circle, then a curved line
between them. And then she writes THE SELF I HAVE BECOME
INSTEAD along the line veering off from the first, and THE ARC
OF UNFAITHFULNESS along the curved line.

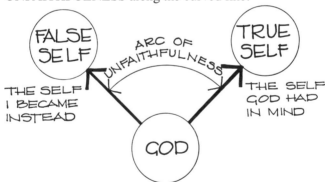

In the deepest dimensions of ourselves we are made for communion with God. We are drawn by a profound longing inward
toward, and then outward from our sacred center. But a false self
veers off, crafting an ego, a fascination with pretense, the contrived,
the one-dimensional. This false self becomes obsessed with image
and impression, negating and subverting our inborn relationship
with God. Sharon writes FALSE SELF in the new circle.

Sharon's words bring to mind a teaching of Jesus: "Woe to you, scribes and pharisees, hypocrites!" Seven times in Matthew 23 Jesus introduces his scathing assault on the Jewish ecclesiastical hierarchy with these words. Some scholars interpret "hypocrite" as an image from the theater, meaning "actor," a "maskwearer," one who hides his or her true identity and substitutes a role and script in its place. Poignancy, however, more than anger, may best characterize Jesus' words. "Woe" is more closely akin to sorrow than wrath, and later verses in the chapter remind us that Jesus' deeper longing is to gather these temple leaders under his wing, as a hen would gather her brood.

Like an alcoholic who heads to the store to buy bread but ends up at the bar, like a school boy who vows to complete his English assignment but watches television instead, we were birthed to become ourselves but end up somewhere else as someone else. Provided with home and love, we end up in a far country. Sent to Nineveh, we sail for Joppa. Like Paul, what we promise to do, we do not; and what we vow not to do, we do. Called to loyalty and prosperity, we end up in Babylon. Shunning transformation, we remain conformed to the world. Graced with a garden, we end up east of Eden.

Sharon next suggests that we are confronted with two choices, given that "arc of unfaithfulness." Option one is to CLOSE THE GAP. We can try to get back on course on our own, to return to faithfulness by an act of will. I can decide to lose five pounds, drink less, or stop smoking. I can stop bad habits and start better ones. I can read a book, attend a seminar, find a therapist, tap various self-help resources, and make important and significant changes. People can. And congregations can. Sensing it has lost its bearings or gotten off course, a local church can spruce up the building, liven the newsletter, buy new choir robes, or plan new programs, and things may change.

When initiative and creativity, plans and strategies can work, we should use them. But, as life too often testifies, our efforts often just do not and perhaps cannot work. Ask anyone whose diet plans, resolutions to stop smoking, and promises to change have failed. Ask congregational leaders who have created a long-range plan, brought in an experienced and respected consultant, attended leadership training seminars, followed dutifully what were promised to be foolproof church growth strategies, only to find that little changed. Sometimes alteration and adjustment, initiative and effort alone work for ourselves or the church. And sometimes a more dramatic change, change of a different and more radical nature, is called for.

After providing another opportunity for individual and silent reflection, Sharon returns a last time to her diagram and makes a long, sweeping line in red marker. This is the JOURNEY HOME, which Merton suggests is threefold:

1. *letting go of the false self,* the persona, the mask, the personality we have so carefully crafted, knowing it is not the "person God had in mind when he created us," and acknowledging that we have lost our way and cannot find our way back as an act of will;
2. *falling downward into God,* where we (re)discover the true self, recover our sacred center, reclaim our "true name," our "self hidden with God in Christ";
3. *emerging outward* toward living a life more faithful to our truer self, never perfectly or completely, but daily retracing this journey to and through and from our sacred center.

This choice, the transformational choice, is the more awesome choice. Merton writes:

To anyone who has full awareness of our "exile" from God, our alienation from this inmost self, this claim can hardly seem believable. Yet, it is nothing else but the message of Christ calling us to awake from sleep, to return from exile, and to find our true selves within ourselves, in that inner sanctuary which is his temple, and his heaven, and (at the end of the prodigal's homecoming journey) the "Father's house."[9]

---

This journey needs to focus on spiritual disciplines, our commitment to devotion and prayer, as well as on our "marketplace life," how we live as a truer self in our everyday routine.

The classic *The Cloud of Unknowing*, a little book written by an unknown fourteenth-century English mystic, speaks of a "path of effort" and a "path of surrender," and may offer some insight into the blend of intentionality and surrender needed for this journey. The early pages of this spiritual classic challenge the reader to courageous, dauntless effort in spiritual pursuit. But recognize, this anonymous writer counsels, when effort has come to its limit, when intention can take you no farther. Finally, the anonymous author argues, "lay a cloud of forgetting" over all that effort has yielded, and over effort itself. Then, he pleads, stand before the "cloud of unknowing," beat upon that "cloud of unknowing," bow before that "cloud of unknowing" until the way forward opens.[9]

Gerald May, a psychiatrist who works with Shalem Institute in Washington, D.C., has written a contemporary parallel, more a text than a devotional guide, called *Will and Spirit*. May distinguishes between "willfulness" and "willingness," and the urgency of discerning the difference between the two. People are understandably inclined first toward *willfulness*—purposefulness, setting and achieving goals. Life does, indeed, challenge us to creativity and resourcefulness, responsibility taking, problem solving, and meaning making. But we become driven by compulsion, slaves of a need to master and manage life. Willfulness must yield to *willingness*, to surrender and trusting—a movement for which we have neither practice nor inclination.

Finally, the journey home requires great faithfulness and trust, especially for those times when fear interrupts and intrudes. This is best illustrated by one of my favorite stories. Terry and Barbara had spent six months in London as part of Terry's training in thoracic surgery. Taking advantage of a Monday holiday, they planned a three-day weekend near Brighton, on the coast. An operating room technician, hearing about their plans, told Terry about a very special and little known beach in that area. "This is the most beautiful beach you can imagine," she said with a lilt in her voice. "If you want to go, I'll give you directions."

"Absolutely," Terry replied.

"Listen carefully. Take notes. Write exactly what I tell you," she instructed. "Take the main road south into Brighton, then head west along the coastal road," she began, speaking slowly so Terry could record the precise route. "Go exactly 14.7 miles, look for a gravel road to the left, and turn in. Drive six-tenths of a mile more, and park by the large oak tree. Walk about, let's see, fifty paces. You're kind of short, Terry, so maybe fifty-five paces. Look to your left and you'll see a cavelike opening in the side of the steep hill. Walk through the cave and it will bring you to this exquisite beach. Trust me. It's worth the effort."

Terry and Barbara packed the car, tucked their young sons, Jamie and Greg, in the backseat, and headed south. They reset the trip odometer as they made the turn onto the coastal road, found the gravel road at exactly 14.7 miles, turned, drove another six-tenths of a mile, and parked by the oak tree. Sure enough, at the fifty-fifth pace they found themselves standing at the cavelike opening. They grabbed the picnic basket and beach towels, ready to press their toes into the sand and sample the ocean.

They walked briskly, at first, along the path that led down a gentle slope from the mouth of the opening. The light diminished as they walked, so they slowed their pace. With each bend in the passage-way, the light continued to dim. Suddenly they took a rather sharp turn and found themselves in total darkness. Jamie reached for his father's hand, Greg grasped his mother's, and they stood still. "Maybe we ought to head back and find the public beach" was the thought on all their minds, they would later admit when they reminisced about that moment. But they remembered the promise of an utterly magnificent beach. So they began to edge forward, searching for steady footing as they went. The darkness continued for what seemed no doubt longer than it really was. Then, as they eased around another bend, a whisper of light danced on the pathway ahead. Slowly their pace quickened again, and moments later they emerged onto what was, they all agreed, a beach even more beautiful than they had imagined.

The journey to the sacred center is a lifelong exploration, and we seem at times to pass through moments of darkness and fear. We are tempted to turn back, to opt for the safer and more familiar. Or, inspired by a promise, uncertain as we may feel, we can reach for one another's hands and keep walking. My spiritual director once told me, "Each prayer can renew your surrender to God, your relinquishment of ego, your dying to self, your crucifixion with Christ. And each prayer can renew your resurrection, celebrate your new personhood in Christ, your rising with Christ." Each day we can release into the hands of God the work and plans, hopes and dreams, accomplishments and failures, joys and disappointments of the day, inviting God to return them upon awakening in a renewed and redeemed form. This is recovering the sacred center every day.

*Part Two*

# Theology and Metaphor for the Sacred Center

A generation ago a major denomination had established an extensive missionary presence in central Africa. One particular compound included a chapel, school, health clinic, and community center. Individual homes had been improved, a basic sewage system installed, and a community well dug. Leaders of this compound, in consultation with their denominational leaders, decided to send a team to develop a new mission station some distance to the south. Using primitive maps and local guides, they plotted a three-day trek through the jungle to the targeted area. It seemed a demanding but reasonable plan.

The first morning, before dawn, the contingent of European missionaries and African porters set out. They arrived on schedule, just after sunset, at the anticipated first day's destination. They pitched their tents, prepared a basic meal, ate quickly, and went to bed. They arose in predawn darkness, ate a hurried breakfast, packed the gear, and headed out again. The terrain was steeper than anticipated and the underbrush along the trail thicker than expected, but they arrived at the end of day two at the planned location. Utterly exhausted, they ate quickly and pitched camp hastily, knowing it would be a short night.

They arose the third day before dawn, confident they were on target to arrive at their ultimate destination by nightfall. The missionaries arrived at the center of the camp to find the porters sitting on their packs, clearly not ready to depart. "We're not going one step further," a spokesperson said, "until our souls catch up with our bodies."

The life of faith and the call to leadership can become frenzied and fragmented. There is so much to do. Issues and people, tasks and agendas, reading lists and endless meetings beckon, often clamor, for our attention. There are problems to solve and conflicts to resolve, letters to write and phone calls to make. There are not enough hours in the day, and our bodies race ahead of our souls.

Part 2, "Theology and Metaphor for the Sacred Center," provides the groundwork for an alternative to giving seemingly endless attention to tasks, responsibilities, and demands. It explores the interface between Scripture and experience (chapter 3), proposes key elements of a theology of the sacred center (chapters 4 and 5), and demonstrates the value of uncovering new metaphors for describing what the sacred center means for daily life and ministry (chapter 6).

*Chapter Three*

# Living and Telling the Story
## New Metaphors for Theological Process

I did not like geometry, and I did not like the geometry teacher, Mr. McDonald. I think he knew it, so he looked surprised that warm June afternoon in eleventh grade, when I stayed in my seat after the bell had rung and the rest of the class had left. I bent intently over my notebook, and my pencil pushed furiously across the page. I was on to something! Mediocre math student that I was, I dared to believe that I was on the verge of something momentous. It all began with idle doodling, drawing circles, playing with numbers—and a hunch.

"What are you up to?" mumbled Mr. McDonald, as he peeked over my shoulder.

"Give me a second," I muttered, engrossed in my page full of numbers. Suddenly it all was falling together. This is clearly break-through work, I thought to myself. "There's this number, Mr. McDonald," I said breathlessly. "I'll have it in a sec. Let's see. If you multiply this number times twice the diameter, it gives you the circumference of the circle!" I said proudly. I was too busy to see the smile on Mr. McDonald's face. He didn't say anything. "Wait," I rushed on. "If you multiply it times the radius ... hm-m-m ... wait a second ... times the radius of the circle squared, it gives you the area of the circle." Now I was honing in. "I've just about got the number, Mr. McDonald," I blurted out, enthusiastically. I thought I would explode as the endless rows of numbers were about to yield

45

the bottom line, the magic number. I read the numbers slowly as I wrote them: "Three point one four." My voice caught in my throat. A rush of embarrassment surely reddened my face.

I looked up sheepishly at Mr. McDonald, but he had the broadest smile I had ever seen on his usually lined and grumpy face. He could have walked away as soon as he had seen the folly of my work. My attitude in class to date might well have justified a sarcastic comment. But instead he said, "Congratulations. You've experienced math for the first time. You've tasted the joy of the inventor. Yes, I know, I understand. You've only discovered pi, but math, education, and learning will never be the same for you." He was right.

## Discovering Theology Together

To differing degrees and defined in differing words, Christian churches hold the Bible as a source of unique inspiration and high authority. The pages of Scripture, our most direct available link to sacred history, emerged from firsthand, eyewitness experience of the biblical drama as it unfolded. Centuries of scholarship and reflection have yielded a legacy of theology as well as ancient and modern creeds that offer concise explanations of cornerstone Christian tenets and define denominational orthodoxy.

This has been a rich, living, and dynamic process spread across countless generations. A liability of theological discourse and doctrinal creeds is, however, that they can become fixed and static, one generation's template force-fit on another generation's reality. Sometimes theology closes the borders, discourages further exploration, and declares that the last word has been spoken. When Christians speak theologically, they often become distant, mechanical, and dispassionate. Their words become strained and their sentence structure awkward. Clergy or laity, they become artificial and inauthentic. Theology and life seem to disconnect as they talk. Speaking becomes speech making and anything but intimate. Theology becomes real and life-giving when concepts become a matter of conviction, when theology is discovered as well as taught. That demands personal involvement, participation in the theological process, and shared ownership of truth. Theology belongs to the people, as we "discover pi" together.

If we are to challenge Christians to go deeper and recover the sacred center, we need a fresh and dynamic approach to relating to the Bible. The graphic below evolved from a circle of Sunday school leaders at Gladwyne Church. A small circle of parents, discouraged by their children's disinterest and even active resistance, decided to reinvent Sunday school. They chose an open classroom, activities-based approach. That decision meant two things. They would have to write their own curriculum, and they would develop a basic approach to understanding the Bible, because they wanted the lessons to be biblically based.

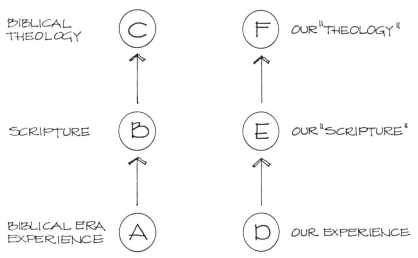

On the left: Circle A represents the experiences of biblical writers. What did these writers see and hear in person or receive from those who were eyewitnesses? What did they think and feel in the midst of that experience? How did the experience affect them? Something happened and they responded. Circle B represents biblical passages, reports in written form of those experiences, words no doubt influenced by the personal reflections of the writers and transmitted orally for decades. Circle C represents the corpus of biblical theology and attempts to look comprehensively and systematically at the full biblical text and to identify foundational truths. The arrows are drawn, appropriately, upward.

This schema is admittedly simplified. Redaction criticism reminds us that the editing process is as important as the writing process in forming biblical text. Sociohistorical criticism reminds us that the faith experience of the early church became a lens through which the historical events of Jesus' time were viewed. The movement is not as simple as A to B to C, but it will work for our purposes here.

On the right: Circle D represents our experiences. What do we see and hear in person? What firsthand experiences do others share with us? What do we think, and how do we feel? How do our daily experiences shape us? Circle E represents our search for meaning—our reflections, interpretations, conclusions. Much of this we carry within us, unwritten and often unspoken. But in safe moments we share these reflections with others. Some of us write them down, often informally as diaries and journals. These musings and interpretations, thoughts and feelings become our "scripture." Finally, circle F represents our worldview, our basic interpretation of life, our assumptive system. This may remain largely informal or unconscious. Paralleling the development of formal Christian theology, we evolve a personal theology, formally or informally, as we live and reflect on our lives. Again, we draw the arrows upward.

The goal of the Sunday school was to place the living experiences of the biblical writer in dialogue with our own. They asked, by what process can our life experience be illumined and transformed by that of the biblical witnesses?

Such an approach might seem foreign to some contemporary preachers. A vast majority of ministers claim to base their sermons on the Bible. Curriculum writers and local church teachers do the same. "We are a Bible-preaching, Bible-teaching, Bible-believing church," boasts a sign outside a nearby church. But this claim may be unrealistic, inaccurate, even deceptive, because inevitably Scripture is viewed through a theological lens positioned between the preacher and the text. Theology calls this hermeneutics, a set of assumptions about Scripture that define a normative approach to a given biblical text. These lenses can sharpen our focus, or they can confuse and distort.

A sermon is never simply and unambiguously "what Jesus said and what he meant by what he said." It reflects as well what the preacher thinks or what those who have most influenced the preacher think Jesus meant. I do not mean this as indictment. I mean only that preachers need to acknowledge this process more forthrightly. Whereas a biblical text is once removed from the experience of the writer, theology is twice removed. I am suggesting that the typical movement in preaching and teaching is (in terms of the graphic) downward from a particular theological perspective (Scripture viewed through the lens of a prior biblical theology considered by the preacher or teacher to be valid) then to the worshiper or student. This seems to me to be one possible interpretation of the given passage but not necessarily the only possible interpretation. The arrows, reconfigured, indicate the flow of this largely inductive homiletical and educational process.

## A New Lens

There is another choice: crafting new lenses in order to look *downward*—to look beneath and behind the biblical text into the experience that animated it. This can become, then, a shared exploration—"looking downward" toward the living and life-giving, meaningful and meaning-giving, real-life experience of the biblical characters and authors, and "looking downward" into our own life experience. This process opens the possibility of a unique and vital partnership with biblical characters, a shared search for understanding and meaning, a dialogue between journeys and journeyers—at the level of experience. The flow of the arrows shifts again.

I am convinced that people in the pews are longing for permission and encouragement to embark on this kind of theological adventure, with clergy and laity becoming partners in this exploration.

BIBLICAL
THEOLOGY            ◯ ⟵------⟶ ◯        OUR "THEOLOGY"

SCRIPTURE           ◯ ⟵-----⟶ ◯        OUR "SCRIPTURE"

                    EXPERIENTIAL
                       LENS

BIBLICAL ERA
EXPERIENCE          ◯ ⟵----⟶ ◯        OUR EXPERIENCE

This journey means acknowledging forthrightly both the gifts the limits of theology itself.

To a degree, theology is inevitably, indeed, wonderfully autobiographical. Our minds long to penetrate objective truth, but this truth is always and inevitably received and shared subjectively. Even revealed theology is carried in the earthen vessels of human language. I can speak only for myself. My perception, experience, and description of truth is known only through the lens of my life story.

Someone once said at a couples retreat that praying together is more intimate than making love That sounded outlandish, until I gave it some thought—no, until my wife and I decided to start praying together! It turned out to be more intimate and awkward than I would ever have expected. I am discovering a parallel in sharing with you my personal theology. As a pastor and teacher, I frequently share theological reflections, but sharing my essential worldview, my basic assumptions and my core theology as a single piece, makes me feel somewhat vulnerable.

Fortunately, theology is process more than finished product, journey more than destination, truth discovered along the way, revealed as we go. Much becomes known only in retrospect, upon reflection. Theology seems forever provisional, tentative, and incomplete. Language has its limits. Any attempt to communicate deep truth requires groping for symbols and images. People approached Jesus with questions, but he answered with stories and riddles. His images and symbols can seem mystifying and baffling. Linguists remind us that any given word points, labels, defines, and identifies something—but is not the thing itself. Theology, as Eastern thought suggests, is like a finger pointing: We look not at the finger but at that toward which it points.

## The Limits of Language

Italo Calvino writes:

The struggle of literature is in fact a struggle to escape from the confines of language; it stretches out from the utmost limit of what can be said. What stirs literature is the call and attraction of what is not in the dictionary.[1]

So it is with theology. Although it can be meaningfully expressed through language, language cannot fully contain it. I love and respect language. "Preachers," an artist friend once told me, "are choreographers, sculptors, and painters with words." Knowing the limits of language and then daring to explore the frontier just beyond them is the challenge and adventure of theological pursuit.

Imagine ten or twelve of us sitting together in a comfortable living room around a large round coffee table, struggling together to explore the relationship between experiencing "deep things" and the means of communicating those experiences.

Imagine all available means of communication heaped onto this coffee table. Piled high on the table are all the words and phrases of our language—some sixty thousand items, linguists tell us. But there is more. The language of *sound* is piled there as well—music, voice and instrument, laughter and crying, shout and groan, grunt and sigh. The language of *movement* is there—dance and gesture and expression. The language of *color and form* are there as well—sculpture and mosaic, symbol and image.

Now imagine this broad array of means of communicating not merely piled on this immense table but arranged in a certain way. Think first only about the words and phrases of written or spoken language. Toward the center of the table are the words and phrases of clearest and most exact definition, those words around which there is high consensus of meaning. As we move toward the edges of the table, words and their usage become less clear, more imprecise.

The closer we come to the edge of the table, the greater the degree of uncertainty. We find the right word more quickly at the center of the table, while we search more carefully at the edges.

Language toward the center is literal and uncomplicated; language toward the edge becomes symbolic, employing metaphor and analogy. We would find prose toward the center, poetry toward the edge; legal documents toward the center, love letters toward the edge; discourse at the center, humor toward the edge; Newtonian physics toward the center, quantum mechanics edging outward, chaos theory hovering at the edge.

As we move toward the outermost limits of language, we begin to struggle, falling ultimately and inevitably into silence. When the language of word and phrase has reached its limit, the language of the nonverbal arts is born. The languages of sound and movement, of color and form begin to speak. But these, too, reach their limit. Movement falls into stillness, sound becomes mute, color and form yield to the inexpressible. There is no more language. Yet there is more to be said.

Now, imagining that it has a glass top, peer through the table, looking downward. This downward view represents seeing, understanding, experiencing life ever more deeply. It is here that we find insight, gratitude, awe and wonder; and connecting.

The Christian faith affirms that life invites us to experience and live with ever-increasing depth. To whatever degree we have been graced by the gift of forgiveness, we can know that gift even more fully. We are coaxed to experience the ever more beautiful, the ever more truthful, the ever more peaceful, the ever more joyful, the ever more loving. "Whatever is true,... honorable,... just,... pure,... pleasing,... commendable,... think about these things," Paul instructs us in his letter to the Philippians (4:8).

Paul stretches toward the edges of language as he writes to the Romans. What knows the depth of God? he seems to ask. Then he quickly suggests an answer: the *Spirit* of God. What knows the depth of a person? he ponders. The *spirit* of the person, he continues. His exact words speak to the heart of the matter: "God's Spirit joins himself to our spirits to declare that we are God's children" (Romans 8:16, GNB). In our depths, recovering our sacred center, in "sighs too deep for words," our hearts touch and are touched by the very heart of God.

Life and faith beckon us ever deeper toward the center. Yet, thinking we have plumbed as deeply as we can go, we are drawn deeper yet. Such is the wonder and mystery of the life of faith. "For I received from the Lord that which I also delivered to you," Paul reminds us (1 Corinthians 11:23, RSV). Logic and reason can take us only so far; then the Spirit takes us farther yet.

Whenever we touch and are touched by deep things, something in us longs to share that truth and joy. At times this deepening perspective can be expressed clearly, in center-of-the-table language. More often, however, our experiences from this increasingly deep place drive the search for words outward toward the edges of the table, to the frontiers of language. Picture an ever-widening angle—as it goes deeper, it also goes wider.

Tertullian, a fourth-century theologian who gave as much shape and definition to our faith as any early church father, wrote a line often quoted in the original Latin, *fides quaeres intellectum.* Understanding *(intellectum)* can seek *(quaeres)* faith *(fides),* but ultimately only fruitlessly. Paradoxically, only faith can birth understanding. Logic and reason can lead us only so far.  Anselm, one of the early church's most prolific theological writers, began each major section of his work with this disclaimer: "Remember, I can say nothing that is true about God."

Simply stated, the more deeply we experience faith and trust, peace and joy, love and forgiveness, grace and truth, the more we are pushed toward and beyond the edges of language, where language becomes more uncertain, poetic, and symbolic. And the more we insist on clear, literal, center-of-the-table language,

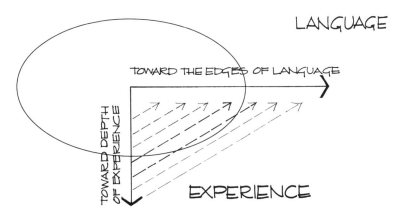

the more we discourage exploration of depth and the adventure of fresh discovery.

## Risking New Language

I believe that Christians everywhere are longing for a personal invitation to look deeply, to break new ground, to risk new language. They want to recover the sacred center and then to explore at the edges of language in order to give voice to their discovery.

A group of seven newcomers gathered in my office for the next session in our new members' program. The evening's theme was basic Christian beliefs, and each member opened his or her notebook to a fresh page and got ready to write. I would teach and they would take notes.

On a whim I said, "Write down three beliefs, or four or five, that you hold with passion, that you find life-giving." Then I waited a moment. No one lifted a pen. "Was I unclear?" I asked. "No," they responded, "we're just trying to figure out what we're supposed to write."

I found that a troubling response, a sad indictment of the failure of the church to invite true spiritual exploration. Sensing that encouragement might set them free, I assured them, "It's not about what you're supposed to write but what your heart wants to write."

Group members began, hesitantly at first, to scratch a line or two across the page. Then the momentum picked up. Lines became paragraphs, then pages, penned with increasing energy. "Finished?" I asked after ten minutes. They kept writing. After twenty minutes, then thirty, they wrote on. I finally had to insist that they stop and begin sharing.

People began to talk, and the sharing was profound and touching. Having received permission to write, they gave one another permission to speak. The conversation was animated, with hearty laughter and quiet tears. Not a single person around the circle had been a stranger to the presence of the divine, not one life untouched by the sacred. Some used familiar, traditional language. Others chose new words, fresh analogies, untried metaphors appropriate to their unique experience. All spoke with sincerity and personal power. And all that I might have said in a lecture on basic Christian beliefs, and much more, was spoken. All of the seven commented that they had never before been invited to share in their own words what they believed. Each of them had held deep, personal, passionate, and life-giving beliefs for years but had never felt invited, or safe enough, to speak them at a church.

What they demonstrated is the intensely autobiographical nature of theology, and that theology grows out of the dialogue between biblical characters and experience. This act, one movement of recovering the sacred center, invites us to plumb the depths and eventually to dance at the edges of language.

*Chapter Four*

# Temenos

## A Theology of Sacred Space

My wife and I live at a retreat center named Temenos *(téh-men-ohs),* which is Greek for "sacred space." I did not like the name when I first heard it. The sound of it fell rather harshly on my ears. But all that changed one quiet October afternoon a few years ago.

I went for an afternoon walk down the gravel lane that runs in front of the farmhouse at Temenos. The day had been busy, but I felt my mind quiet and my body relax as I walked. About a mile down the road I happened upon a house painter climbing down his ladder for a midafternoon iced tea break. With an exchange of nods, I joined him. In the midst of our conversation I mentioned that I lived at Temenos down the road. "Oh," he said, his eyes opening wide, "you live at a temenos. How wonderful."

"You live at *a* temenos," I repeated, with obvious curiosity. He was Greek and seemed delighted to tell me just what a temenos is. He explained that when a village is founded in Greece, the elders and wise ones discern where the temenos ought to be, where the ground is holy. Nothing is built there—no houses, no public buildings, not even a church. It becomes community space. Villagers may bring plantings or wooden benches, perhaps stepping-stones or small statues, but only to nurture the sacredness.

Then his explanation became particularly compelling. He said that when villagers feel discouraged, upset, or confused, they go to the temenos, sit quietly on the grass or by the stream, and find that their mood suddenly shifts. When people from the community find themselves arguing or speaking harshly to one another, they move their conversation to the temenos, sit on a bench or walk a path together, and find themselves speaking with greater respect. They begin to talk and listen more carefully, and soon their conflict resolves. When people have a decision to make or feel uncertain or torn, they go to the temenos. After a quiet, solitary moment in an open field or under the shade of a stand of trees, their mind suddenly becomes clearer. "Ah, such a perfect name," I mused as I walked back home. "Temenos is just that, *a temenos*."

Church, before it is a geographical location or even a gathering of people, is a quality of time and space. Before it is worship, program, and organization, it is climate, tone, feeling, and atmosphere. It is, or tragically it is not, sacred space, holy ground, sanctuary—a quality of place. It is, or is not, sabbath, *kairos*—a quality of time.

Ernest Gordon, a predecessor of mine at Montauk Community Church and retired dean of the chapel at Princeton University, tells a moving story of the creation of a temenos on the River Kwai during World War II.[1] Gordon was an officer in a unit of Scottish Argyles interned in a Japanese concentration camp on the Burma-Thailand border during the war. As a Christian and ranking officer, he wanted to inspire courage and faith in the face of awesomely brutal and dehumanizing conditions. The bitter cold of winter set in and the ravages of disease, particularly typhoid, took their toll. Food portions became more meager, a salty gruel for breakfast, a crust of bread and a cup of water at lunch, a thin and meatless soup for supper. Meanwhile, work on the infamous "railroad of death" over the River Kwai became more intense and physically assaulting. Gordon watched as courage, determination, faith, and resilience, including his own, ebbed. Some began to steal food. As a countryman would edge toward death, others would hover, ready to grab his blanket, threadbare work suit, or worn boots as he breathed his last. Faces that had once been alive with courage were now lined with fear and suspicion. Once spirit is broken, Gordon writes in his commentary on the experience, the body will soon die as well.

In a last attempt to maintain compassion and respect, someone suggested that each man have a buddy, a special friend, someone to look after. No one took the idea very seriously, except Angus McGillivray. Angus's buddy got sick and did not have a chance, everyone quietly concluded. As they watched, with increasingly vacant stares peering from tragically depleted bodies, Angus's buddy began to get well. Angus would feed his buddy the tiny allotted portion, then add his own. Angus would tuck his buddy's thin blanket around him, then add his own. Slowly his buddy gained strength and returned to health. Then, one night, Angus died.

Ever so slowly, almost imperceptibly, something began to change. Something lost began to be reclaimed. Some new spirit began to emerge. Suddenly, as Gordon tells it, a church came into being. This church had no walls, no doors, no windows, no stained glass, and no altar. No mortar was mixed and no stones were set in place. No boards were cut and no nails were driven. Yet everyone knew exactly where the church stood. Entrance doors were just to the right of the mess hall, and the altar was just in front of the wash house. First one, then others, began to nod gently as they passed through that entrance "door," and to bow, perceptible only to knowing eyes, as they approached the "altar." Though an invisible church, it became a very real church—a nurturing and nourishing, safe and comforting, stirring and empowering church.

The camp was liberated before a single stone or board was put in place for that church. Doors, pews, windows, or altar were never constructed, yet a church existed, one that bore the features of all that a church essentially and most truly is. I first read Ernest Gordon's telling of this story during my first six months of ministry. I made a commitment, as a parish pastor, to work to form that kind of church.

That commitment to parish ministry had begun decades ago in the midst of an event that more than any other would mold and shape my life on every front. In the spring of 1955 I was fourteen years old. My mother, who had fallen on the steps of our summer house the year before, complained of pain and stiffness in her shoulder and neck. Medication, traction, and special exercises had not helped; the pain had worsened and she became sad and discouraged. Surgery was suggested, and although the family physician advised against it, it was scheduled.

I left for school the morning of my mother's surgery with no anxiety, at least none that I can remember. I called before I took the bus home, and something in my uncle's voice stirred alarm in me. "Maybe something went wrong," I wondered. "Don't be silly," another voice in my head answered, "she's fine." The internal dialogue continued as I sat alone in the back of the bus. I walked up the long hill from the bus stop to our corner. My dad was standing at the curb. I felt my heart pounding as I ran toward him. "She didn't make it, Howard," he said, and he threw his arms around me and held me tight.

My life collapsed. I cried as each friend came to visit and I cried through dinner. I felt lost and confused and sad and lonely. After supper, folks from the church began to come by. Uncle Joe and Aunt Betty, Uncle Carl and Aunt Margie, Uncle Clint and Aunt Millie were not really my aunts and uncles, but I called them that. The people at church were like our family.

Then the minister arrived. After talking with the folks downstairs, he came up to my room. "Your bus from school goes right past the church," he said, after we had talked for a while. "Any time you want to, if you see my car in the driveway, just hop off and come on in." Many afternoons I did just that. Mr. Cosline felt safe. He cared about me, listened to me, and affirmed me. His office felt safe, and so did the rest of the church.

Six months later a woman at the church asked me one Sunday, "What do you want to be when you grow up?" I wasn't much past the fireman, policeman, or baseball player age. "A minister," I heard myself say. I was as surprised as she was! From that day, now forty years ago, I have never questioned my sense of vocation. I finished high school to go to college to go to seminary to become a parish minister. Looking back, I would guess that because the minister and the congregation were so loving and supportive of us, I decided that I wanted to do the same for others in the future. There was something about the church, the pastor, and the people—and something about the way I felt when I was there with them. It was more than what they believed or how they worshiped or things they did. It was a feeling, a tone, an atmosphere. It was a quality of time and place that I now call temenos.

For several years I have led four-day contemplative retreats titled "In Search of Sanctuary and Sabbath." I find the metaphors of the psalms to be nurturing, inspiring, and empowering—God as "strength," "very present help in trouble," and "refuge." God as

"protector," "safety," and "dwelling place." God as "sanctuary." In
some passages this experience or feeling of sanctuary occurs within
literal, actual, physical sanctuary. In the majority of these passages,
however, "sanctuary" is not physical. It is invisibility, mystery, in
a certain sense only an imagined place—yet very real. Constructing
visible sanctuary does not necessarily create or capture Spirit but
must rather be filled by Spirit. Perhaps a spirit of sanctuary is
discerned, and then physical sanctuary is built around it. The
psalmist seems to long for this experience of sanctuary within
physical sanctuary.

The mystics, ancient and contemporary, are helpful in exploring
these metaphors of sanctuary, holy place, and temenos. Reading
and pondering the mystics, it seems to me, demands a certain
indirection, a willingness to dance with ideas, to appreciate the
poetic and, at first glance, the obscure. The mystics speak in richly
varying ways of a "place" of communion, of union, of oneness with
the divine—a real place, yet a "place-less place." Teresa of Avila
wrote of an "interior castle," inviting those on the mystical path to
spiral ever downward toward that deepest chamber within, where
one is truly at one with God. Thomas Merton imaged this interior
sanctuary or communion with God as a "palace of nowhere." Like
the prophets and Jesus, these mystics, separated by four centuries,
lamented the degree to which physical sanctuary and institutional
church did not manifest, or nurture, this kind of holiness. And they
longed to call the church to renewal.

## The Word *Contemplative*

Brother David Steindl-Rast is a living mystic, a Benedictine
monk who has written and lectured extensively on the contemplative life. English being his second language, Brother David has a
curious and endearing appreciation of and insight into our language.
His exploration into the word "contemplative" is engaging and
illuminating. He points out that Stonehenge, that remarkable and
mysterious stone monument in England, is aligned to the point of
sunrise at the summer solstice, then to other points of rising and
setting of both the moon and sun through their cycles. "This small
part of earth is patterned on the heavens. Order observed above
gives rise to order realized below. Here lies the key to the meaning
of Stonehenge. It is the key also to the meaning of contemplation,"

Steindl-Rast observes.[2] He then proceeds to unpack the word *contemplative*.

ConTEMPlative: "temp," a notch, a primitive mark of measurement; "temperature," a measurement of heat and cold; "temperament," a measurement of psychological style; "to temper," to measure ingredients carefully. More significant, though less familiar, is another word from this same root, *templum,* from which comes the word *temple*. Though most commonly associated with architectural form, an earthly construction, a temple's more ancient and primary reference was "sacred precinct in the sky." In ancient times the seers, augers, prophets, and priests contemplated invisible, heavenly sacred form. "Again and again the Bible emphasizes that Moses built the tabernacle precisely according to the pattern that had been shown to him on the mountain," Steindl-Rast writes.[3]

ConTEMPLATive: "template," a series and sequence of measurements. From a simple assembly guide that locates where to place nails or screws to elaborate architectural drawings for a public building, a template arranges measurements into a meaningful pattern. Whether following the contours of the tabernacle or the contours of the faithful life written on tablets of stone, Moses urged those who followed him to pattern earthly reality after the heavenly intention. In the most ancient and primitive sense, form follows function.

ContemplaTIVE: "tive," one who embodies. This tiny suffix suggests we are called to be ones who divine and discern heavenly intention. To argue that sacred intention exists is intriguing but hardly meaningful. To seek to discern divine will is the call.

And finally, CONtemplative: "con," a prefix meaning "with" or "together with." We are reminded that merely gazing at the vision is not contemplation at all. That might at best deserve to be called "templation." Contemplation joins vision and action.

I find people everywhere, inside and outside the church, longing for this quality of place—sanctuary, holy ground, sacred space, temenos.

## Kairos

The spacial metaphor of temenos finds a parallel in the temporal metaphor of kairos, the sacredness of time. Unlike English, which has only one word for time, biblical Greek has two: *chronos*—

chronological time, time marked and measured with a clock or calendar; and *kairos*—fullness of time, meaningful time, ripe time, God's time. Rabbi Abraham Heschel, in his book *Sabbath*, explores this sacredness of time in ways that delightfully echo the reflections of the psalmist, Teresa of Avila, Thomas Merton, and Brother David Steindl-Rast.

Heschel points out that most religions are dominated by a notion that deity resides in space, and thus they are more inclined toward the sanctity of place—sacred mountain, holy city, sacred shrine, holy monument. God is conceived primarily as thing, not spirit; God can be located and contained. Heschel insists, however, that the Bible is more concerned with time than space. The "God of Israel," he writes, "was the God of events: the Redeemer from slavery, the Revealed of the Torah, manifesting himself in events of history rather than in things and places. Thus the faith in the unembodied, in the unimaginable, was born."[4] Judaism is a religion of time aiming at a sanctification of time.

Heschel suggests an order of creation, what he calls a "hierarchy of holiness"—sanctity of time issues from the Creator first, then the sanctity of humankind and the nation of Israel, and only then the sanctity of space. "The meaning of Sabbath is to celebrate time rather than space ... on the sabbath we become attuned to *holiness in time*."[5] He notes with sadness that the vast majority of Jewish festivals have physical objects at the heart of their observance—unleavened bread, the shofar, the tabernacle. But no ritual object is required for keeping the Sabbath. "Symbols are superfluous: the sabbath itself is the symbol."[6] He writes in the epilogue of his book:

> Time, that which is beyond and independent of space, is ever-lasting; it is the world of space that is perishing. Things persist within time; time itself does not change. We should not speak of the flow or passage of time, but the flow or passage of space through time.
>
> Time is like an eternal burning bush. Though each instant must vanish to open the way to the next one, time itself is not consumed.... Time is the process of creation, and things of space are the results of creation.... Time is perpetual innovation, a synonym for continuous creation. Time is God's gift to the world of space.
>
> Eternity utters a day![7]

Steindl-Rast's appreciation of the nature and nuance of language yields subtle insight into the concept of sacred time. Noting, as I have, that Chinese creates language with pictures, he reports that the word/picture for "busyness" combines that for "heart" and "killing," and the word/picture for "leisure" combines "spaces" and "sunshine." Many church leaders, clergy and lay, know too well the heart-killingness of busyness, overgiving, burnout, and fatigue. And they long for spaces with sunshine! Speaking English as a second language, Brother David recognizes subtleties of our language we may fail to appreciate. He points out, for example, that we tend to use the words "purpose" and "meaning" as if they were synonyms. Purpose, he observes, is active, assertive, and intentional; purpose is a matter of effort. But meaning calls for a certain passivity, a watchfulness, a readiness and receptivity; meaning is a gift to be received.[8]

## Seeking Temenos Within—
## An Exercise in Imagination

I have asked hundreds of people—in formal and informal settings, in workshops, classes, and private conversations—to join me in the following exercises. I invite you to linger with each step to experience them for yourself. First, you will need to use your imagination.

*In your imagination, create a time and place—a setting, an atmosphere, and a quality of time where you feel safe and relaxed, where there is no reason to be anxious, no facade to hold in place, no image to project or protect. An actual place may come to mind, but feel free to create a brand new one.*

*Imagine a time and place where you can simply be, where you feel strangely and wonderfully at home, a place where there are no obligations and nothing to prove. In this place, you respect and love yourself and others. You are not afraid. You feel forgiven and forgiving, accepted and accepting. Your mind is clear; there is no confusion. You feel held in the hollow of God's hand. Feel*

*the rhythm, energy, and gracefulness of this time
and place. Relax. Do not rush. Sit quietly until
you see this place in vivid detail. Let yourself become fully present there. Then allow yourself all
the time you need to enjoy the gifts of this time
and place you have created.*

*Now, remember a time and place when you ac-
tually experienced the qualities you have been
imagining. Moments when you were alone, away
from others and the routines of the day, may
come to mind first. But add to those memories
"temenos moments" you shared with at least two
other people. An event, or perhaps several
events, may come immediately to mind. Do not
work at remembering. Let the event come to you.
As it does, let it unfold in your mind's eye. See
the faces of those who were present. Remember
the physical setting. Bring to mind the tone, the
feeling, the atmosphere that was present. Do not
rush. Take as much time as you want to savor the
remembering. Then pause for a moment to name
and appreciate the qualities that characterized
the moment.*

I have yet to encounter a single person who has not brought to
mind, rather quickly and easily, special moments in time when "it
happened"—sometimes recently, sometimes years, even decades
ago. People retell their stories with energy and animation, speaking
with vividness and vitality, while others listen with unusual attentiveness. Frequently, people linger over particularly poignant parts
of their stories to weep with appreciation and joy. Life has been
generous, they conclude, offering places and moments of sacredness and grace.

Temenos moments occur on docks, in ski lodges, and on beaches;
in kitchens, living rooms, porches, and backyards; in waiting rooms
and locker rooms, at lunch counters and in bars; in buses, automo-
biles, trains, and airplanes; in offices, parking lots, and cafeterias;
in therapy groups and at AA meetings; in chance meetings and at
scheduled events; in fleeting moments and during long, leisurely

hours. A recent college graduate wrote this in his journal after one group's sharing

> It was during finals my junior year in college. We'd been cram-
> ming hard for over a week. We were exhausted. The sounds of
> packing up echoed up and down the hall. Parents would arrive
> with station wagons and vans early the next morning. Someone
> must have heard me crack a beer and soon four or five guys were
> clamoring into my room. It was just a break, I thought. I had so
> much to do. And we were all dog tired. Rick pulled an album
> from my half packed CD collection. Danny kicked off his shoes.
> Marv flopped down on my bed. They were gonna stay awhile.
>   Then . . . "it happened." Hard to say just when. Or how. Or
> why. Or just what the "it" was. They had tumbled into my room
> about 9:00 pm. Suddenly it was 3:45 am! No one had left. We
> didn't tell jokes. We didn't reminisce about the school year.
> We didn't chat about summer plans. Or next year at school.
> We talked. Suddenly, we didn't have to be tough guys.
> Macho. We didn't have to be cool. In ways we never had
> before (and, sadly, haven't much since) we really talked to
> each other. Danny talked about how painful it had been to be
> ditched by his girlfriend back home, after he'd been faithful all
> year long. Marv talked about his dad's illness. We'd not known.
> Or hadn't heard him when he tried to tell us before. We certainly
> didn't know he was dying. Marv, halfback on the football team,
> Mr. Composure, street kid from a tough part of the city, wept.
> Tony shared how and why this had been the best year of his life.
> He'd arrived last fall, shy, hesitant, and uncertain. Somehow he'd
> found himself. Decided to believe in himself. We could see it
> now, in his face, in his eyes!
>   For the longest while, before we finally dragged off to bed,
> we stood in a circle just hugging each other.

Rich are the qualities and characteristics remembered and appreciated in those temenos places and kairos moments: peacefulness
and unhurriedness, attentiveness and mutual respect, openness and
trust, caring and compassion, forthrightness and integrity, genuineness and trustworthiness, safety and protection, a celebration of
commonality and diversity, laughter and tears, sound and silence,
a sense of God's presence, being present to each other, mindfulness.

People often notice as they conclude their sharing, however, that
few of the remembered moments occurred in church or a church-
related setting. Frequently someone adds, rather hesitantly, that

they do not really expect them to happen in church. "When I am at church, or with church people," someone will typically comment, "I feel more on guard, less open, more careful."

Many confess, tragically, that they find church an unlikely place to nurture such experiences: "When I walk into my church I find myself tighten. I feel more on guard, rather than less." "When I first came to this church I felt quite open and I spoke quite freely, but that wasn't such a good idea. Eyebrows raised. Things I shared in confidence became public information and community gossip. I'm more careful now." "My AA group, my therapy group, my support group, that's where I feel at home, safe, trusting, and open. My church? No way!"

These are all too typical remarks—coming largely, remember, from church members! This woman's observations are all too typical:

> Every once in a while "it" happens at church. Especially when we have small groups. Bible studies, book groups, a couples' group. Someone starts to be personal. Share something. Risk something. Then someone else does the same. I'm a little slow to open up, but sometimes I can feel myself getting ready. But then someone will change the subject. Or someone will give some answer or solution to what was being talked about. Or someone will make a joke. Or say we were getting off the topic. And "it" will end.

*Return, now, to the events you remembered, the sacred moments, the temenos places, and gently ask yourself, Why did they happen? What was it about the setting or the time that contributed to creating the moments? What did others say or do that created or enhanced the moment? What did you do that played a part? Take the time you need to ponder your response. Give it some careful thought.*

In my experience, responses to these questions fall into two categories. First, we hear about *grace*. "Nothing 'made' it happen; it 'just happened.'" "It was a gift and it was just wonderful." "Praise God, it just came, visited, descended." These thoughts often come

to mind first. These treasured memories seem to have been a gift
from God.

"But grace has to be noticed, welcomed, received," someone will
typically say. "The angel of the Lord appeared in the flame of the
bush," someone once added, "but Moses had to notice, to take off
his shoes." Eli told Samuel to say, "Speak, Lord, your servant
hears." But it is up to us to say yes to the voices that stir in the night.
Jesus the healer walked by, but Bartimaeus had to cry out and claim
the moment.

The second category of responses, then, is about *effort*. Upon
closer examination and deeper reflection, people do begin to remember who did something that welcomed, enhanced, enabled the
gift of grace. Without relinquishing their appreciation that the
moment was a gift of grace, they recognize that intention, specific
and nameable behaviors were also significant. "I did open the door,
and Rick did pick the right CD," that college student remembered.
"Danny opened up and risked his sadness, and Marv talked about
his dad. That broke the ice."

As they give it careful thought, people remember the attitudes
and behaviors that tend to invite and welcome, if not create,
temenos moments. The first person to take a risk, to share something personal, and the way the group responds seem crucial.
Acceptance and nonjudgment are named as key ingredients. Some
blend of passivity, of not forcing the moment, along with desire and
commitment seems essential. The way the group handles a first
confrontation, a sharp difference in opinion, is seen as important.
Will "wrong answers" be tolerated? Are there "wrong answers"? Is
it okay to be different? a dissident? offbeat? Some mix of patience
and persistence seems vital.

I spoke in chapter 2 of *The Cloud of Unknowing,* written by an
anonymous fourteenth-century English mystic, which invites spiritual pilgrims to persist as far along life's path as effort and determination can lead, then to lay a "cloud of forgetting" on effort and
stand before the "cloud of unknowing," the cloud of grace. I spoke
as well of Gerald May's distinction between "willfulness," that
which intention and commitment can yield, and "willingness,"
appropriate surrender to the grace-filled gifts of the moment. In the
concluding pages of *The Road Less Traveled*, Scott Peck suggests
a simple formula: COURAGE + WORK leads to GRACE.[9] Grace

cannot be planned or scheduled. Temenos moments cannot be announced for a particular date, time, and location. Perhaps courage and work position us for grace.

And so it seems that paradox is at work—a weaving of intention and grace. This is a delicate balance. Time and space, it turns out, are not neutral, not merely context, background, or scenery. Time and space are not some empty stage onto which we walk as actors to speak our lines. Much like the air we breathe, time and space have quality and substance—nourishing or toxic, healthful or harmful. Parish leaders who will lead the way toward a reinvented future church must tune in to this longing of the human heart for sacred space and sacred time. They must discern the moments when temenos and kairos, the gifts of grace, seek to break through and break in. Such leaders know they cannot create it, mandate it, will it, or compel it. They can only sense it, embrace it, and be embraced by it, bow to it, delight in it, and celebrate it.

Temenos and kairos stretch our imagination and our language. At their heart, they are mysterious, elusive, and mystical. They defy definition and elude mere strategy and manipulation. The winds of temenos and kairos blow where they will. But if the church is not first sacred space and sacred time—if parish leaders are not its guardians—little else matters.

*Chapter Five*

# Emerging from Within
## A Theology of Person

### Created from Sacred Center

When I was five we lived in a Civil War–era house in Philadelphia. In my parents' bedroom was an old-fashioned vanity. I loved to pull out the bench seat that was tucked underneath, scramble up on my knees, prop my chin on my fists, and gaze into the three hinged mirrors, the outer ones turned slightly inward. I would lean forward and twist to one side so I could catch a glimpse of the back of my head. I was fascinated.

And then I would lean still farther, until my nose almost touched the glass, and peer into my eyes. I knew that those small black circles at the center of my eyeball were where I looked out from. I looked into the reflection. Who's in there? I wondered to myself. I remember that scene vividly and often. Fifty years later, while straightening my tie or brushing my hair, I still lean forward, peer into those little round holes, and wonder, Who's in there? A very short poem comes to mind: "I? Why?"

The search for identity and self-understanding seems universal. It is a quest, as captivating as any, that both accompanies and energizes our life journey. Who am I? Who are you? What is our essential nature? What are we meant to become?

If we had been attentive and well behaved, my third-grade teacher, Mrs. Franklin, would end the day by reading us a story.

One day she sat down and said, "I'm going to read a story called 'The Lady and the Tiger.'" It went something like this.

In some country in the middle ages a man had committed a crime serious enough that it could not go unpunished. The judge, rather than demand a fine be paid or a jail term served, devised an unusual and ingenious sentence. On a warm and sunny Saturday afternoon, as the townspeople gathered in the village square, the man was confronted by a small building with two identical doors. The structure was simple but without windows, so no one could see what was inside. "Behind one door," the judge explained, "is a beautiful woman. If you open that door, she will step out to be your wife. Behind the other door," he continued, "is a huge and hungry tiger. If you open that door, the tiger will leap out and devour you."

Mrs. Franklin looked up and found all of us sitting very quietly. She went back to reading. "The man stepped up on the platform in front of the doors. The boards creaked as he stepped toward the knob of his choice, and the latch squeaked as he began to turn it." Mrs. Franklin slowly turned the page as we all held our breath. "The end," she said quietly, and closed the book. "Was it the lady or the tiger?" we shouted, almost in unison. "I don't know," Mrs. Franklin said, as she turned and held up the last page so we all could see it. It really did say "The End." "What do you think?" she asked. No one said anything.

I do not know who wrote that story or what the author had in mind. But I have come up with my own meaning. If we could approach the portal that leads to our truest and deepest self, turn the knob and open it, who would emerge? Perhaps beauty, truth, light, wisdom, and love. Perhaps destructiveness, falsehood, darkness, and hate. Likely some blend of the two. Some who hear and reflect on the story suggest a third door behind which there would be, simply, nothing. Their deepest fear, they confess, is that emptiness lies within.

One way to mark the stages of my spiritual journey is to track my struggle with a single verse from the Sermon on the Mount, in which Jesus says, "Be perfect, even as your heavenly Father is perfect" (Matthew 5:48). My father had been raised as a Methodist and imprinted with Wesley's "doctrine of theoretical perfectibility." My child's mind translated that simply, "If you *can* be perfect, then you *should* be perfect." My father meant this Methodist spin to be challenging and encouraging, but that was not its impact on me. No achievement, no matter how noteworthy, could approach perfection; no effort, no matter how ardent, could hit the mark. Jesus' words became discouraging and self-defeating to me. That verse hung around my neck like the proverbial albatross for two decades.

My first year in seminary I heard a preacher talk about the incident from John's Gospel about the adulterous woman (John 8:1-11). This story functions as a great leveler. "Anyone out there perfect?" Jesus asks. And led by the elders, the angry accusers walk away. "There, that's settled," seems to be the teaching. No one is perfect. That preacher had no idea the sigh of relief I breathed.

Years later, Auburn Seminary professor Walter Wink focused on this verse at a retreat I attended. I found I was not alone in my struggle with that verse. Many among us had found it downright intimidating. Walter let us share our struggles, then simply stated, "Jesus could not have said that!" Having our immediate attention, he went on. "There is no word for 'perfect,' at least as it relates to people, in the language that Jesus spoke. Hebrew thought and language knew better than that. 'Be shalom,' perhaps," he said. "'Be compassionate' or 'be loving,' but not 'be perfect.'"

Recently, another perspective has blended with these others: not "be perfect" but "you are perfect." The human being—beneath all that hides the fact—is perfect, a child of God, a precious treasure. We bear the image of God; we have been inbreathed by divinity. At our sacred center lies God-ness.

## A Theology of Sin: Losing the Sacred Center

Sin is variously defined in the Bible. The creation story highlights disobedience, defiance, and rebellion; the prophets focus on idolatry and injustice. "Transgression" defies a moral code, "trespass" evokes territorial images, and "debts" is a financial allusion. The Old and New Testaments alike suggest both "estrangement" and "missing the mark" as cornerstone themes in defining sin. Jesus, who offers little direct teaching about sin, focuses more on sins of omission than commission. Surely sin is anything that separates us from God, one another, and ourselves. I offer as another definition of sin "losing the sacred center."

My Jewish mystic friend Raquel spoke one day about a class she was teaching at the church. "I am a sinner," she said intently, leaning forward in her chair. "Ask anyone in my family. Ask my friends. They know best. They are the ones I have hurt. They'll tell you. I am a sinner." Then she paused. She gently placed her hand on her heart, and her voice got quiet. "But I am not a sinner," she said. "In my deepest, truest self, the self that God made, I am perfect." She was not offering a concept to debate. This was not theological discourse. This was the way Raquel experienced the way she behaved in the world (the sinner) and yet the self she know in her heart of hearts (the perfect child of God).

"You're just soft on sin, Howard!" I was often accused when I tried to interpret this theology of human nature. Anything but, I hope. Sin entraps and enslaves, distorts and destroys, invades the body and darkens the heart. It perverts and separates. It is falsehood and deception. Paul says, "I don't do the good I want to do; instead, I do the evil that I do not want to do" (Romans 7:19, GNB).

Four metaphors capture the tragedy of sin—metaphors that seem faithful to the biblical witness, grounded in life as we know it day to day, and stepping-stones to forgiveness and redemption.

## Sin as Disguise

It has been years since Floyd Patterson was heavyweight champion. One night at Madison Square Garden in a stunning upset he was beaten by an unknown Swede named Ingemar Johanssen. Reporters and photographers crowded at the dressing room door, waiting to interview the two fighters. Johanssen emerged first with his broad Scandinavian smile and answered questions in broken English. An hour later the last people exited the arena, but no one had seen Patterson. The dressing room was empty.

The defeated champion, it seemed, had disappeared. He did not return to his home, and they could not trace his car. A week went by. Finally, hesitant and embarrassed, the defeated fighter returned home. "I couldn't face them," he told his wife to tell the press, "so I put on a disguise and slipped right by them that night." In an interview years later Patterson revealed that this had been his strategy for years. He had become a master of disguise.

Adam hid his face, and Cain tried to hide. Jacob ran away to elude his brother's wrath, and Jonah sailed to Joppa. Elijah raced to Horeb to escape the threats of Jezebel, and Moses tried to backpedal from the call of the burning bush. The woman at the well hid behind lies, and Nicodemus, the cautious rabbi, hid under the cover of night. A frightened man hid his talent in the ground, and we hide our light under a bushel. And Floyd hid behind his disguise.

There is an ironic sadness to finding the "perfect hiding place" when we play hide and seek. You feel safe and successful. No one can find you. You won't have to be "it." But the sounds of laughter and play are heard only at a distance. You feel clever but lonely.

## Sin as Forgetting

I suspect the following story is apocryphal, but I share it nonetheless. Jason had just turned three and had a new baby sister. He did not seem jealous, as his parents had feared, only curious, gentle, and loving. One evening his mother had tucked the baby under her blanket, turned on the crib-side monitor, and returned to the living room. "Mommy, can I go talk to my sister?" the boy asked. "By myself," he added. His mother glanced toward his dad, who nodded a cautious yes, and the child headed upstairs.

His parents turned up the volume on the monitor. They wondered just why Jason had made this request. They heard the floor creak as the three-year-old edged toward the crib. The silence stirred their anxiety. Then they heard him speak. "Megan," he said, curiosity in his voice, "tell me about God. I'm beginning to forget."

No word in the Old Testament challenges the people to faithfulness like *remember.* Moses and the prophets recounted the Exodus drama, and Jesus instituted the Lord's Supper. And no word indicts people like *forgetting.* "The Israelites did what was evil in the sight of the LORD, forgetting the LORD their God" (Judges 3:7). "Remember and do not forget how you provoked the LORD your God to wrath in the wilderness" (Deuteronomy 9:7). "So be careful not to forget the covenant that the LORD your God made with you" (Deuteronomy 4:3). "I will not forget your word" (Psalm 119:16, one of nine references to forgetting in the psalm). Wooed by the world, distracted from pathways of faithfulness, we forget God.

## Sin as Blindness

In *Binding the Strongman,* a study of the Gospel of Mark, author Ched Myers notes that noticing the positioning and juxtaposing of passages is key to understanding Mark's portrait of Jesus and his ministry. As a case in point, Myers cites the pivotal location of the healing of blind Bartimaeus (10:46-52). More than simply a particular beggar healed of physical blindness, Bartimaeus, he concludes, is the paradigmatic disciple. The twelve and other would-be followers of Jesus have remained in blindness, but this stranger, this "no name" (Myers reminds us that "Bartimaeus" is in fact no name at all but means merely "son of Timaeus"), "receives his sight" and "follows him on the way." Blindness, Myers concludes, is a metaphor for unfaithfulness and stubbornness, for "slowness of heart to believe."[1] Thus the question raised by this healing story is, has your blindness been healed?

## Sin as Inauthenticity

Of all the metaphors, sin as being inauthentic is the most compelling and powerful. Sin is more than "being bad," larger than simply immoral and unethical behavior. Sin is more than the private, interior evil on which Jesus focused in the Sermon on the Mount. Strangely, sin can be inauthentic goodness, living a contrived morality, being dishonestly ethical.

To be a killer, a thief, or a rapist is sinful. To be racist, unjust, greedy, and prideful is sinful. To be callous and unloving is sinful. To behave in these ways, or to think these things in your heart, is sinful. But is it also sin to *pretend* to be kind, to behave in a caring manner but with a cold and callous heart? Is it a sin to become a lawyer to satisfy your parents' desires or to make a handsome salary or to make a name for yourself, when your heart calls you to be a teacher? As was painfully pointed out to me in a session with a marriage counselor, even spouses can deceive one another by hiding true feelings and opinions under the pretense of being "thoughtful." My wife emphatically agreed that when I communicated with her she preferred honesty rather than deception!

Not unlike others in my profession, I have a long history as a "people pleaser." People find me approachable, affable, and pleasant. I am generally viewed as confident and capable, as thoughtful and caring. After all, my name is Friend! To a significant degree those things are, I genuinely believe, true. But all too often I speak words of kindness through a mask and express my competence through a practiced persona. I find myself sounding like a computer voice mouthing prerecorded lines, mindlessly reciting a memorized script. I become less present and real, more contrived and false.

No two fingerprints are or ever have been the same. Each one of us is a one-of-a-kind child of God. Just as our individual patterns of DNA cause cells to form our particular physicality, some inner and singular integrity and intention, like spiritual DNA, expresses itself in a unique person and personality. To revisit Thomas Merton, the "true self," the "self God had in mind," our sacred center, wants to express itself as authentically as possible as "outer self." But we become "conformed to this world" and take on another, what Merton calls "false self."

We become like those computer-driven, amazingly real robots at DisneyWorld. Those life-size characters were first programmed by running wires from a real person to the corresponding part of the robot. The real person speaks and gestures, synchronized with a recording of the speech, which activates and programs the same motions in the robot. A computer "remembers" the words and gestures and is then able to reproduce them. So I, when captive to sin as inauthenticity, learn and replicate words and gestures "taught" by the world.

Similar processes are at work psychologically, mentally, and spiritually. Created to know and live my unique story, I come to live another story. Eric Berne, who developed the theory of human personality called Transactional Analysis, writes about a "life script," which begins to be formed between ages five and seven. A five-year-old watches the "players" on the "stage" of his or her young life speak their "lines" and notices the "stage directions." There is dialogue, plot, and drama. This child begins to discern the "script" of this play, with its recurring themes, patterns, and outcomes. And, most poignantly, the child begins to learn his or her "part," how to speak the "lines" and follow the "stage directions." The child becomes an increasingly good actor and less and less a real person. Decades go by and the child grows into adulthood only to live like a producer-director, recruiting players, assigning roles and lines, dictating stage directions, managing dialogue, and directing outcomes—all to replicate and perpetuate the "script" learned years before. The person has forgotten his or her own unique and authentic story.

Neurologists remind us that mental processes form in a similar manner. Beginning with the most rudimentary mastery of language, a child begins to collect information, to commit increasing numbers of facts to memory, to think thoughts and exchange ideas. In time the child develops the capacity to interrelate and integrate information, to form clusters and complexes of thoughts. Neurological pathways begin to form and patterns of thinking emerge. Slowly but surely a worldview takes shape, a set of cognitive maps and mental models crystallizes, an increasingly complex and ordered set of basic assumptions coalesces. Between ages twelve and sixteen, based on limited information and incorporating unreflectively the biases of family and teachers, this worldview tends to finalize and harden. We may collect more data, even think new thoughts, but we do not change our basic way of thinking.

Finally, we establish a rather fixed, unchanging spiritual outlook by age twelve, often at the age of confirmation. Just as a young person is ready more fully to appreciate symbolism, metaphor, analogy, and the subtleties of spirituality, that preadolescent worldview hardens. The vast majority of adults, some would argue, simply have not developed a mental process that can grapple with a truly adult faith.

Of course, we are not merely, inevitably automatons. Yet, sadly, every day we reenact the sin of inauthenticity. We don a mask and live a persona, opt for a false self, replay a long-rehearsed script, and speak well-practiced lines. Yet there remains within— longing to be reclaimed, renewed, and reborn—a true self. We await redemption.

## A Theology of Redemption: Recovering the Sacred Center

The reality and drama of redemption, recovering the sacred center, defies neat categories and bursts fixed interpretation. Paul counsels the Philippians to "keep on working out your salvation" (Philippians 12:2), the verb "to work out" being best translated in the progressive tense. In a fascinating paradox in Galatians 6, he reminds the Christian community that this work is both communal ("bear one another's burdens," verse 1) yet rigorously individual ("all must carry their own loads," verse 5). And so it is that the opportunity to recover the sacred center, to be redeemed, presents itself both to individuals and communities.

## Recovering the Sacred Center—As Individuals

The process of recovering the sacred center can be understood as threefold: (1) discovering the true inner identity, (2) putting off the old and putting on the new, and (3) getting unstuck in order to grow again. I recognize that this scheme is no doubt neater and more orderly than the human reality it celebrates, but the individual journey toward redemption suggests the following.

I believe the following stories will convey the meaning of *discovering true identity*. The first comes from World War I in Austria. A household related to the royal family, anticipating Austria's involvement in the rapidly growing hostilities in Europe, created a plan to safeguard their children, a two-year-old son and six-month-old daughter. These parents asked a peasant couple, the gardener and cook on their estate, to take in the children as their own. They then arranged for this couple to move to another part of the country. The royal couple was at risk and barely escaped the war alive. Three years later, now out of danger, they brought the peasant couple and their son and daughter back home. At first the children did not even recognize their mother and father. It took months for the son and daughter to realize and reclaim their true identity.

The second story comes from monastic lore. John Tauler was a medieval German monk and mystic, a mendicant friar who relied on the generosity of citizens from whom he begged. "Good morning," a man mumbled mindlessly, as he walked hurriedly through the streets of the city, tossing a few coins in the monk's direction.

"And good morning to you," John responded, a lilt in his voice.

"Well, have a good day, my son," said the man, a bit startled.

"I'd not expect otherwise," said Tauler.

"And have a good life," the man added, curiosity having gotten the best of him.

"How could I have otherwise?" came the reply.

"Just who are you?" the man asked.

"I am a prince," Tauler answered.

"You're not a prince," the man retorted brusquely, "you're a pauper."

"Ah, a pauper, yes," Tauler gently replied, "but a prince as well. I'm son of the King, you see, and brother of the Prince." The two found a park bench and talked much of the morning.

Abram knew himself as settled and successful. He had worked hard and earned his retirement. But God had another story, indeed a new identity in mind. He ventured from Ur of Chaldees, walked the journey of faithfulness, and became *Abraham.* Levi knew himself as a tax collector, rejected and despised. An itinerant rabbi asked him to follow, and he became *Matthew.* Saul, a zealous Pharisee, knew exactly who he was. And he knew his mission: to pursue and capture Christians. A light threw him from his horse and a voice challenged him, and eventually he became *Paul.*

In his letters, Paul used the metaphor for redemption of "putting off the old" and "putting on the new." The following story illuminates the ancient teaching.

Cecil B. deMille is best known for his stunning Hollywood productions of biblical themes and is surely most famous for *The Ten Commandments.* A pioneer in filmmaking's special effects technology, he had a flair for the dramatic. His genius filled the screen. But in his personal life he was a quiet and retiring man who enjoyed his privacy and relished simplicity.

Shortly after his wife died he went for a week alone at their rustic cabin, a remote camp set on the edge of a quiet pond in Maine. One afternoon, deMille tucked his fishing rod under the bow of his little dinghy and pushed off from the shore. He rowed slowly toward the center of the lake, pulled the oars over the gunwales, and just sat. After a time the stern of the boat rustled through some reeds toward a far bank of the pond and came to rest. There he sat, saddened by the loss of his wife, yet heartened by the gentleness of a familiar spot, when something caught his eye. A water beetle had wandered up the side of the old wooden boat, tumbled over the edge near the oarlocks, and made its way across the weathered seat that stretched across the boat.

Cecil simply gazed down at the water beetle, treasuring this visit with a new, if unlikely, friend. Then the water beetle seemed to shudder, to lurch a bit this way and that. Then it rolled onto its side and died! DeMille felt a fresh stirring of grief over his wife's death, now mingled with the death of his new acquaintance. The old man remained still. The better part of an hour passed.

Suddenly, the water beetle seemed to stir, to shudder again ever so slightly. Yes, the water beetle was moving! The husk of the water beetle cracked and fell away from its body. And just as suddenly there was a fresh stirring from inside. Emerging from the husk, lifting its wings to dry in the afternoon sun, was a dragonfly. Ah, he remembered, these particular water beetles are the larva stage of dragonflies. With that, the dragonfly took flight.

That little incident, more dramatic, he thought to himself, than even the most stirring of the scenes from *The Ten Commandments,* became a twofold metaphor for him. One was about life after death. He watched the shadow of the dragonfly fall across the water beetles still clustered in the water near the boat and wondered if they had any idea about the new life awaiting them after their "death." His faith in the life to come, that his wife now knew, deepened. But the other part of the metaphor was just as important to him. He himself was being invited to pass through this season of mourning, this "death," into new life. He was being invited to shed the husk that had sheltered his life to this point, that the rest of his life might take flight.

Recovering the sacred center is about water beetles and dragon-flies. It demands that with appreciation and honor, we let go of the old and die, passing through transition to the new.

I offer another story to illustrate getting unstuck in order to grow again. The leaves on our jade plant had grown lush and hearty. New branches had formed each year, as they had since my wife's grandmother first placed the plant on her apartment windowsill a half century before. Then, for no reason we could discern, it stopped growing, and its leaves began to become dull and limp.

Our neighborhood nurseryman, like a country doctor who still makes house calls, dropped by one afternoon. He eyed the plant and finally announced, "It's the pot." He went on: "That jade plant has probably lived in that pot for thirty years or more. But the plant won't grow anymore—in fact, it will begin to die—if you don't repot it. Be careful, though," he warned, "because repotting is a shock to a plant. Expose the roots as little as possible. Don't be worried if it loses a year's new growth or its leaves lose even more luster for a time. It'll take awhile to acclimate to its new home. The plant will be at risk. But you have no choice but to move it to a new pot."

## Recovering the Sacred Center—In Community

God has placed us in community, perhaps redemptive community, possibly a local church. Risking undue simplicity, working out salvation together, as with individual redemption, seems to be a three-part movement—seeing, naming, and uncovering.

Truly *seeing* another person is an art, and it takes an artist's eye. You have to see the statue of David in person to fully appreciate the magnificence and genius of this piece of sculpture. Viewers stand transfixed as they look up at this flawless work. Michelangelo crafted this figure from a flawed piece of marble that no other sculptor would touch. When it was unveiled, someone asked him how he had done it. Michelangelo replied that he simply looked at the marble, saw David within it, and then "chipped away all that was not David."

This theology of persons invites us simply to look deeply. Michelangelo "saw" David in the marble. This theology of persons directs us to believe and affirm that waiting at the sacred center is a "true self" waiting to be seen, per chance recovered. Along the two corridors leading to the statue of David are rows of unfinished works of Michelangelo, some a day or two from completion and others a day in progress, some needing only a final subtle touch and others barely taking form. People are like that: works in progress longing for someone each day to see the potential within and to chip away another piece.

Most Western Christians do not understand or appreciate the traditions and practices of the Eastern churches. If we worshiped in an orthodox church, we would find many similarities between their sanctuaries and those of Western churches. There are stained glass windows and statuary, pulpit and communion table, artwork and candles. But there are no pews. And stretching across the church between the sanctuary and the nave will be a wall, the iconostasis, the wall of the icons.

An icon is a painting of a saint or a central figure from a biblical story. These paintings have a certain flat, two-dimensional feeling unfamiliar to the Western eye. A feature of icons is that the main character peers directly outward, as if seeking eye contact with the observer. As a personal act of worship, the faithful will stand before the wall and meditate on an icon. This meditation is an art form that takes, I am told, years of quiet and patient practice to even begin to master.

In this form of meditation, the worshipers let their eyes meet those of the figure in the icon. Looking not too intently, yet not too casually, this eye contact must be steady, reverent, and expectant. Worshipers practiced in this form of meditation report that suddenly, subtly, mysteriously the eyes of the icon figure seem to draw them in, as if they pass into the life and reality in which this saint or biblical figure is standing. The worshiper seems able to know the figure's thoughts, feel his or her feelings, join the person's stream of consciousness, as if the worshiper were living that moment or event from long ago. Orthodox Christians call it a moment of mystical communion.

The meditation continues when, just as suddenly and subtly, worshipers begin to draw the saint or biblical figure through their own eyes into their life and reality, their thoughts and feelings, their stream of consciousness. The figure from the icon now seems joined in mystical communion with the worshiper in his or her moment in time. The faithful of the Eastern tradition report that this mystical communion happens in such a way that they know one another's struggles and joys, confusions and certainties. They touch one another in their common search for God, even as they celebrate a common knowing of God. Finally, when it is time, the figure returns to the canvas and the worshiper whispers an amen, perhaps to move to another icon.

Esau looked into the face of Jacob after their reunion, their hearty embrace by the River Jabbok. "To see your face is like seeing the face of God," he exclaimed (Genesis 33:10). A woman of the street intrudes at lunch on Simon the Pharisee's home, there to wash Jesus feet with her tears and dry them with her hair. Noting his host's annoyance, knowing how quickly and thoughtlessly he would likely answer, Jesus asked a probing question, "Simon, do you see this woman?" (Luke 7:44).

Jesus, struggling for the energy to speak last words from the cross, chose a single word to capture his desire for John and his mother to care for one another, "Woman, behold, your son.... Son, behold, your mother" (John 19:26-27, RSV). I remember a Good Friday service early in my ministry, when I had been assigned this word as my preaching text. I eagerly went to a commentary to explore the word *behold,* which I expected to be one of those involved, many-faceted Greek verbs. It simply means "to look at," however, as if by truly looking at one another, truly seeing one another, all compassion will naturally flow.

A lame beggar sought alms from Peter and John at the Gate Beautiful, but they chose instead to claim the healing power Jesus had promised them. Before reaching out to help him stand up and walk, "they looked intently at him," and then they said, "Look at us" (Acts 3:4). There seems to be healing and redeeming power in simply looking at one another, truly and deeply seeing one another.

A second way in which community becomes redemptive community is when we *name* one another. In the broadway play *Man of La Mancha,* Don Quixote and Sancho Panza enter a roadside tavern for an evening meal. The barmaid, a buxom, foulmouthed, roughhewn woman, is serving mugs of beer to a raucous, drunken afternoon crowd. Suddenly, all eyes turn to Don Quixote who, with a long and sweeping bow, in deep and dignified tones, greets the barmaid, "Dulcinea, my sweet one." Peels of laughter thunder through the tavern, the barmaid's perhaps the loudest. "Dulcinea? Sweet One? Hah!" bellows a burly worker, spilling his beer. "This is Aldonza."

Aldonza is a good name for her. She speaks and acts like her name sounds, harsh, sharp-edged. Much of the play takes place in this tavern, and with every visit Don Quixote repeats his greeting. Each time Don Quixote calls her Dulcinea, something more of the "sweet one," hidden within her rough exterior, begins to emerge, and Aldonza, the harsh and sharp-edged one, begins to recede. By the end of the play she becomes wonderfully, completely Dulcinea.

Jacob knew himself as deceitful, separated by rage from his brother, and a restless wanderer. But he wrestled with an angel, received a blessing, and walked from that moment with a limp and a new name, Israel (Genesis 32:22-32). Shy and retiring Andrew brought his brother Simon to meet a wandering rabbi he had met by the shore. Jesus looked at Simon and declared, "You are now Peter" ("the rocklike one," John 1:40-42). Those rough and weathered fishermen within earshot likely howled with laughter. "Right, Peter, rocklike, sure!" They knew Peter as changeable, mercurial, tempestuous—anything but rocklike. But Jesus saw within Simon a Peter, a potential, a possibility of rocklikeness, and named it.

Finally, faith communities become redemptive when members invite each other to *uncover* the true self. My wife and I spent an afternoon a few years ago touring the Metropolitan Museum of Art in New York City. We were about to leave the impressionist wing when an artist standing close to a large canvas in a cordoned-off smaller room caught our eye. We ventured around the barricade to watch more closely. At first we thought he had a brush in his hand, but looking more carefully, we saw he was working with a scalpel. He carefully placed the edge of his hand against the canvas, pressed the blade to the surface, and lifted away a tiny piece of pigment.

Our curiosity got the best of us. "What are you doing?" we asked quietly, not wanting to disturb him. He seemed delighted to explain. "I am removing pigment from this canvas," he began. "The painting I am removing is rather fine. Almost museum quality," he went on, "but not quite. An art historian was studying it one day and noticed an unusual texturing on the face of the canvas. The expert concluded this artist painted over an existing painting. It's a long story," he continued, "but further research supported the hunch that the original painting, the one obscured by this one, may have been done by someone later recognized as a master."

He told us that it was not uncommon for a struggling artist, whose paintings had not yet found a market, to sell a completed canvas to be used by another artist as if it were a fresh canvas. Sometimes that struggling artist came one day to be recognized as a master. "As I said, this is a fine painting. But beneath it, we believe, is a masterpiece. To put it simply," he concluded, "my work is to carefully remove what isn't masterpiece so that what is masterpiece can be revealed."

What a perfect metaphor. My false self, my inauthentic and contrived self, my persona or mask may be "perfectly fine," almost "museum quality." It may be a self I have carefully honed and refined, practiced and presented to the world daily. But beneath it may be a masterpiece.

Only a trained eye can spot the signs of a hidden masterpiece, but it took a skillful restorer deftly to lift away the pigment that hides the covered work of art. Only Lazarus could heed Jesus' command to come out of the tomb, to awaken from death and walk into new life, but it was the task of his neighbors and family to unwrap him (John 11:44). Each Christian must say yes to the redemptive work of grace, but companions on the journey may do a vital work of unwrapping and uncovering.

The story of creation, sin, and redemption must become our story. Redemption is a process. It may include dramatic and extraordinary moments, but it unfolds in everyday reality. Redemption occurs in a context. It is inevitably relational. Redemption must be declared as a basic truth at the heart of the Christian message, but it must be also experienced in the heart of believers. The local church, I believe, is rich with opportunity to become more fully such a context. The congregation can become community—sharpening vision, setting goals, making plans, building team, doing ministry—where redemption becomes a real, everyday, and life-giving experience.

*Chapter Six*

# Frog or Butterfly, Airline or Airport?
## Metaphors of Transformation

In nature, transition from one form to another occurs in various ways. The transition made from tadpole to frog, for instance, is a gradual, visible, orderly *developmental* event. By contrast, the transition from caterpillar to butterfly is a mysterious, hidden, startlingly unexpected *transformational* event.

Generally, the development from tadpole to frog can be captured by time lapse photography, making it clear that "what is" came from "what was." If, however, you open the chrysalis a caterpillar has wound about itself, you find only a mass of cells whose ultimate form and function cannot be identified. Although a biologist might not be completely comfortable with this description, we could say the caterpillar disintegrates into cells that must reorganize to become a butterfly. Inside a chrysalis, there is neither a caterpillar sprouting wings nor a husk dropping away to reveal a butterfly. Yet all the caterpillar was and all that the butterfly will become are contained in the chrysalis.

In the case of the frog, basic structure is preserved, used, and expanded, while it remains exposed to the environment. Tadpole-to-frog transition occurs in an essentially organized, orderly, and incremental way. In the case of the butterfly, in a process hidden from the environment by the chrysalis, basic structure is abandoned.

Caterpillar-to-butterfly transition occurs in a more chaotic, dis-rupted, and apparently disorganized way. Both rely on genetic encoding and available energy to make a successful transition from one form to another, but do so in fundamentally different ways.

In the physical world, life demands a source of energy, and transition to new life follows a cycle. All life forms draw and release energy. When energy is available, a season of growth and develop-ment follows. When this supply of energy begins to diminish, life apparently ceases. Often this season of dormancy is followed in turn by a renewal of energy and the life cycle continues.

This phenomenon from the physical world has implications for organizational life. Organizations behave like living organisms. Organizations, including congregations, must draw and release energy and pass through seasons of a life cycle. Congregations that lose their energy or that become dependent on limited sources of energy must eventually wither and die. To flourish, flowers and animals, people and institutions must constantly seek new sources of energy. The primary sources of energy for churches are the people in congregations, those in the world served by the church, and the divine source from which the church receives its life. Life forms that continue to awaken to new growth move through each season of their life cycle by relinquishing one season to allow the emergence of the next.

When contemplating this process of transition in the life cycles of frogs and butterflies, developmental or transformational, I see parallels that apply to congregations, especially to their styles and methods of leadership. These lessons for organizations drawn from physical science seem to me to suggest two basic approaches to leadership and planning. The first, *developmental* leadership and planning, is sequential and incremental. One stage builds upon another. An organization or congregation following this approach may enlarge or downsize as circumstances dictate, reorganize as seems appropriate, but the givens remain unchallenged and un-altered. Developmental leadership can be imaginative and life-giving, yet is inevitably limited, unable to rise to certain challenges and opportunities. This is tadpole-to-frog leadership.

The second approach, *transformational* leadership and planning, by contrast, appears at first glance to be chaotic and sporadic.

Givens are explored and open to alteration. Basic assumptions are examined. This is caterpillar-to-butterfly leadership.

Each leadership and planning approach makes a unique and timely contribution. The challenge is not choosing one over the other but artfully blending the two. Transformation toward the reinvented future church requires a leap of discontinuity. Something must be crossed. At first glance, "you can't get there from here." The process of transformation refuses to be sequential and orderly. Consequently, developmental leadership, necessary as it sometimes is, cannot help the church make the leap. That is the task and gift of transformational leadership.

## Airline or Airport?

A story makes the point more concretely. Over a two-year period the mission and outreach committee of Gladwyne Church made a concerted effort to increase both financial commitment and personal participation in mission projects. The official board endorsed this commitment as a congregational priority for the year. I was asked to preach periodic sermons on the theme. The church school teachers built a mission and outreach element into the curriculum for all ages.

Three mission opportunities were identified in that first year. The committee made colorful posters, wrote engaging newsletter articles, encouraged me to promote the projects from the pulpit, and communicated with members of the congregation to inform them personally about these opportunities. But all this work yielded only disappointing results. In the second year different projects and sites were more carefully chosen, more attention was given to publicity and advertising, and more assertive strategies of encouragement were adopted. But the results were, again, disappointing.

When the mission and outreach committee met to plan year three, Joe, the chairman, suddenly exclaimed, "We're taking the wrong approach! We're trying to be an airline when we should be building an airport." They saw his enthusiasm and heard the energy in his voice, but their faces remained quizzical. Finally, someone asked, "What are you talking about?!"

"An airline," he explained, "tries to coax as many passengers as possible into a limited number of seats on a limited number of flights headed to a limited number of destinations. If your desired destination is not on the airline's list, you don't use that airline," he continued. "An airport, on the other hand, seeks to provide a safe setting for an optimum number of takeoffs and landings for large and small planes headed in a variety of destinations. The destinations are determined by the operators of the planes." Subtle nods suggested they were beginning to understand. "So as leaders," he went on, "we become more like air traffic controllers than pilots."

The committee began to get the picture. That year they chose no sites and no projects for mission involvement but simply asked all members of the congregation to pray and reflect to seek a sense of calling and personal giftedness, to discern where inner purpose and a passion to serve stirred in them. This new approach was a risk, vulnerable to misunderstanding and failure. Over and over, gently yet persistently, members of the church were asked to ponder where and how their hearts might lead them to make love manifest in service. The committee and I offered encouragement and resources to help the congregation with this inner exploration. People were encouraged to share their ideas—at worship and meetings, in classes and informal conversations, wherever they gathered.

Rosalie, a longtime member of the church, stood up one Sunday during worship and said, in her wonderful Southern drawl, "I don't know why, but I have been feeling a persistent calling to work with people with AIDS. I don't know anyone with AIDS. This is not a work I would have sought or chosen. But I've pondered and prayed, and I think God is leading me to this." She invited anyone who shared her interest to meet her after the service over a cup of coffee. To her surprise eight people joined her. "I don't know why either, Rosalie," one man commented, as others nodded in agreement, "but I couldn't wait for Howard's sermon to end and the postlude to start, so I could come and join this conversation." That first conversation launched an AIDS ministry to Calcutta House in West Philadelphia, one of many such initiatives taken that year.

The mission and outreach committee empowered many mission efforts. Over the next twelve years, eighteen mission groups formed. Community gardening was supported in Chester, Pennsylvania. A housing project in North Philadelphia recently received a second HUD grant for $1.5 million. A ministry to the homeless called Trevor's Campaign gained international recognition. A center to support Christian base communities in Haiti was established. A project to provide bicycles for Nicaragua was formed. A housing project, together with an artisans' cooperative, was sponsored in Mexico. An after-school program was created in the Ludlow section of Philadelphia. Mission and outreach financial commitment increased 200 percent during a three-year period! For two consecutive years, giving to special mission efforts totaled over $100,000, in a church with just under three hundred members and an annual budget of $150,000.

Implicitly or explicitly, individual Christians and Christian congregations make a decision about what they understand "church" to be. Some simply maintain loyalty to business as usual, doggedly perpetuating existing forms, denying the ineffectiveness of these established methods, and rejecting new paradigms and their potential fruitfulness. All of us have witnessed the decline and ultimate failure of such churches. These churches do not adapt well to change but cling to merely developmental models of leadership and planning, or no planning at all.

Some church members and leaders, however, may choose a different way, daring to catch a glimpse of a future church that God is calling into reality. These churches tune to an inner stirring and become transformed, joining the adventure that leads toward a renewed church of the future. These churches understand that change is inevitable and rise to meet the challenges and opportunities presented by opting for transformational models of leadership and planning.

Isaiah counseled a people in captivity, "Do not cling to events of the past or dwell on what happened long ago. Watch for the new thing I am going to do. It is happening already—you can see it now!" (Isaiah 43:18-19, GNB). Paul, using his own faith journey as an example, urged new Christians, "The one thing I do ... is to forget what lies behind me and do my best to reach what is ahead" (Philippians 3:13, GNB). The enthroned God in John's vision declares, "Behold, I come to make all things new" (Revelation 21:5, RSV). It is time for the church to "forget what lies behind" and "watch for the new thing that God is doing."

Transformational leadership reexamines purpose, vision, values, and principles of a congregation. This approach requires a rigorous exploration of basic assumptions, mental models, and conceptual maps, a process more elusive than meets the eye. Patience and steadiness are demanded through inevitable periods of apparent chaos. Courage is essential.

All churches need developmental leadership and planning—a clear, effective, and workable infrastructure. In today's culture, however, if that is the only structure available in which to exercise leadership, the members will become disenfranchised and subsequently disenchanted with the church. Churches that remain responsive to the needs of members will encourage more informal, less structured, more transformational planning options—what I call "adhocracy." In an adhocracy, an idea is surrounded with only as much structure as is truly needed.

## Changing Metaphors and Congregational Renewal

I have become increasingly convinced that significant change occurs for individuals and organizations, including congregations, only when the unconscious is accessed and engaged. In my experience, the unconscious responds well to symbols and images. Many churches have discovered metaphors that have helped them change. Let me share a few of them.

I shared the "airline or airport" story with a congregation in a New Jersey seashore community. They found it intriguing but elusive. It stirred curiosity but did not come to life. After one session, a young elder volunteered, "I have a metaphor for us. We've been trying to run a cruise ship, and we haven't done much of a job recruiting passengers. What if we were a flotilla instead? We have lots of boats—sailboats, fishing boats, ski boats, large and small boats. You can rent them from us or bring your own. We'll place channel markers and keep the harbor clean. What do you think?" he asked. A new vision was sparked, and a fresh momentum carried through the rest of the retreat.

Later the metaphor was expanded. "If we're going to become a flotilla instead of a cruise ship," a deacon mused, "then our leaders are harbor masters, not ship captains."

A trustee sitting nearby caught the spirit and began to further interpret the metaphor: "A harbor master provides slips to dock the boats, safe fueling, maps and charts, water skis and scuba equipment and fishing gear, provisions in the ship's store, and a friendly welcome to the dock."

This metaphor became their metaphor, born of their creativity, emerging from their community. It has been inspiring and life-giving for them as leaders and for the larger church membership.

When the leaders of a small Baptist Church in an ethnic community on the edge of Philadelphia heard the "airline or airport" story, it didn't light any fires. An hour or two went by and the story seemed to be fading—until a teenager at the meeting lit up. "It's like those pottery shops, side by side, on Main Street," he exclaimed. "You can buy fine pottery at one, or make your own at the other."

"And it's the pottery workshop that does the better business," an older officer noted.

"I get it," the board chairperson chimed in, "We've been trying to sell fine pottery. What if we became a workshop instead? We'll provide the materials, work tables, paint and brushes, a bake oven. Come and make your own."

This congregation began to risk letting old and tired programs die, then took a greater risk yet. They stopped trying to create new program offerings, at least in the old model. They began instead to make themselves available to their community. They reimaged their church building as a workshop, a place to be creative. They provided tools and resources, but the people were invited to come and pursue their own calling, develop their own program or ministry. A declining church with a questionable future began to turn around.

In another church, an older woman observed, "We've been trying to get more players into the game, but we ought to get more games on the field."

"What are you talking about?" the pastor asked.

"You weren't our pastor then," she began, "but about eighteen years ago the township created a park and built a soccer field. It became very popular. And soon you just couldn't get any more players into the game. So they put more games on the field! Games for little kids and big kids and adults."

"And not just soccer," an elder remembered, "but tennis, volleyball, baseball."

Another church leader remarked, "I think the most ingenious decision the township made was building that huge equipment locker. Mitts, bats, and balls; volleyball balls, nets, and chalk to draw the lines; badminton racquets and birdies; even puzzles and board games to play inside. And they invited the community to bring their own equipment to store and share."

Their life-giving metaphor was born.

A large church in a growing city in Pennsylvania was making a transition from the era of a long-term, beloved, but rather autocratic pastor to a new era of more partnership-based leadership. "We have to get clear about what kind of church we want to be!" an elder declared. "But we have so many different ideas." She seemed to be right. Differing visions seemed to be colliding. There was fear that these competing ideas would fracture the church. They talked about whether they might be a department store, a home center, a giant hardware store, or a huge food store.

Finally, the Christian education director suggested, "Maybe we ought to be a mall."

The others picked up her metaphor. "You're right, Jean," was the consensus. "A mall has two or three anchor stores, like worship, and children's education, and pastoral care. But it has lots of smaller stores and specialty shops," the senior pastor said, building on this fresh idea.

The staff brought this new metaphor to the official board, which brought it to the congregation. The mall metaphor affirms variety and multiplicity, yet is a coherent and cohesive image as well. It has helped tap the ever broadening energy of this growing congregation in collaborative and mutually supportive ways.

## Finding Your Own Metaphor

I believe the continuing viability of the local church depends on an understanding of the concepts presented in this chapter, or something like them. Change is upon us and the time for transformation is now. I often ask leaders of congregations just how much change, how much chaos, how much of the unexpected and unpredictable they are ready to tolerate, or even welcome. When I truly lay down the gauntlet, I ask if they would be willing to see their church, as they know it, go out of existence so a resurrected church might emerge.

When we talk about true transformational leadership, I believe we are talking about what some faith traditions call "paschal mystery," the mystery that lies deep in the heart of the crucifix-ion/resurrection event. Paul challenged the Romans, "Do not con-form yourselves to the standards of this world, but let God transform you inwardly by a complete change of your mind" (Romans 12:2, GNB). He writes to the Corinthians, "When anyone is joined to Christ, he is a new being; the old has gone, the new has come" (2 Corinthians 5:17, GNB). Paul's images for baptism speak in similar ways (Romans 6:5-14).

Many churches may have failed to seize the moment. Indeed, the moment may have passed them by, and they may now have become embarrassingly ineffective, even irrelevant. I believe, however, that the local church can be a place of transformation.

*Part Three*

# Becoming a Transforming Congregation

One congregational leader coined a fascinating phrase. "I call it the 'sowing/reaping paradox,'" he said. "I sow here—turning the soil, planting in straight rows, watering and weeding. Then I watch. Time passes, and something catches my attention out of the corner of my eye. I see buds and blossoms, flowers and fruits and vegetables, over there—an unexpected harvest. Sowing here, then, illogically, reaping over there. And somehow knowing, strange as it all seems, sowing and reaping are related."

"Nothing happens if you don't plan," added another church officer, "but don't expect what you planned to necessarily happen. In fact, expect something even better!"

Part 3, "Becoming a Transforming Congregation," is about sowing and reaping, making and changing plans and doing the work of ministry in the local church—"working as if it is all up to us, and praying as if it is all up to God." Chapter 7 introduces the metaphor of church-as-a-person and outlines a strategy for exploring the identity of that person. Chapter 8 presents through story central issues for leaders of a transforming church. Chapter 9 explores ways to affirm, tap, and mobilize full congregational potential. Chapter 10 names five core elements—people, team, values and principles, charism, and vision—and a threefold model of leadership: inspiration, consultation, and celebration. Chapter 11 offers a fresh and practical approach to visioning, planning, and action taking.

*Chapter Seven*

# The Church-as-a-Person
## A Metaphor for Exploring and Planning

As we begin to address more practical matters, there is one more metaphor to explore. This image arose in what only later came to be remembered as a significant moment for our congregation. Leaders of Gladwyne Presbyterian Church were on their annual retreat, and Walter Wink, a New Testament professor at Auburn Theological Seminary, was the leader.

As I reflect on it now, I wonder whether the planning process for the weekend perhaps had as profound an effect on the church as did the content. A special committee of the board had invited Walter. I would have concurred with their choice—but I was not asked! A subcommittee designed a brochure for the event. In the past I had created these brochures, but this time I was not consulted. The weekend inspired, it turned out, a larger turnout than in prior years, and the evaluation forms indicated that an important reason was the brochure.

This subplot of shifting power and changing leadership patterns thickened through the weekend and into the years ahead. Church leaders were consciously working to flatten the hierarchy, relate more as peers, and work with less dependency on the clergy staff. Though I fully concurred with its goals, in the midst of this process, I must confess, I often felt awkward, uneasy, and threatened. Sometimes I felt free to share those feelings. Just as often I kept them to myself. We had made a clear commitment as clergy and lay leadership to make the transition from dependence to inter-dependence, from clergy dominance to shared decision making and partnership. But talking about it was far easier than doing it!

Early in the retreat, after an icebreaker and introductions, Walter asked us to get together with two other people and decide together how we wanted to introduce Gladwyne Presbyterian Church to him and to each other. The guidelines were simple. We were to picture the church-as-a person. That meant giving the church-as-a-person a name and describing him or her. What does he look like? How does he dress? What are some of his habits? What are her favorite activities? What energizes her? We were also asked to list some characteristics or traits of this church-as-a-person. What adjectives might describe her personality? What are some positive qualities that make him appealing? What are the negative traits that are not so endearing about her? Our final task was to think of what advice we would give the church-as-a-person.

People were hesitant, confused, and resistant at first. But slowly the small groups became animated and the introductions became both fascinating and revealing.

After a break, Walter led us in Bible study. We explored the creation story, noting that institutions and organizations, as well as human beings, are part of God's creation. Political, social, and economic structures are more than just background for the human story. These structures are an integral part of the drama of creation.

We studied a passage from the prophets and became aware that the prophets challenged not only individuals but political, judicial, and economic spheres as well. We concluded our biblical reflection with an in-depth examination of Colossians 1:15-20, observing that among what was created "in, through, and for Christ" were *thrones* (seats, offices, locations of people of power), *dominions* (the sovereignty, authority, essence of power), *principalities* (locations, jurisdictions, realms of power), and *powers* (the authentications, constitutions, documents of power).

Walter concluded the evening by commenting on two themes that were the focus of his most recent work. The first offered a concept that the social sciences call "corporate or collective personality," the idea that groups of people, especially under certain circumstances, act as if they were, in fact, a person. The second theme was related to the phrase "the angel of the church," taken from the opening line of each of the letters to the seven churches found in chapters 2 and 3 of Revelation.

When we returned in the morning, we began to delve into those seven letters to the churches in Revelation. Walter pointed out that, contrary to what appears to be the case, the word "you" in these verses is almost always singular. This singular "you" refers to the "angel" of the church, which in turn refers to some "collectivity" of the total community, as if the "angel" represents the whole of the church. Walter suggested a phrase that would come to have meaning for us, that the "angel" was the "within-ness," the soul, of the collective personality of the church.

Again working in small groups, then in the total group, we developed a rather detailed description of our church-as-a-person. We tried to be honest. We wanted to appreciate the endearing qualities of our church but also to name its negative qualities. Everyone seemed defensive at first, as if desiring to protect the church from criticism or attack, but we decided that candor and forthrightness would be most productive. As we worked, it became more and more natural to regard our church-as-a-person. We began to discern its angel.

The logical next step was to ask the question, How can we change the church so that we can protect and deepen the positive qualities and begin to eliminate the negative ones? Momentum built as we brainstormed ideas. Then a psychotherapist from the group spoke up, commenting that if the church really *is* like a person, change is not going to be all that easy. After all, it is not easy for us as individuals to change. Another therapist from the group built on the idea, noting that when people want to change and try their best but do not change, that means that their unconscious mind has taken control. No matter what the conscious mind has decided, when what you *actually* do is quite different from what you *decided* to do, that is because your *un*conscious mind thought, felt, remembered and planned differently. What we discovered through this conversation was that if we wanted to change our church, we would have to get access to its unconscious. And in order to do that, we would have to learn its story.

During the last hours of the retreat, we began to explore the history of Gladwyne Church in search of the formative events that had shaped the church-as-a-person we knew in the present. We recounted eras of glory and retold stories from eras of pain. We remembered times of joy and noted times of sadness. We wondered out loud, as if talking about a close friend, what it would take to fully claim the gifts and heal the wounds of that history. We felt a fresh affection for the church, a keener awareness of who it was, what made it tick. We shared a deeper bond with the church, more empathy and understanding. We experienced stronger loyalty to the church, a more durable commitment.

As the retreat came to a close, Gladwyne's leaders began to plan ways to carry this exploration into the whole congregation. They decided to fan out into the congregation, at that time about 225 members, seeing themselves not unlike the "remnant" of the Old Testament or the "leaven" of the New. The goal was to involve as many members of the church as possible. Five groups met separately for half an hour to clarify their mandates. Group one would explore the church's past, its history and legacy. Group two would explore the church's future, its call to ministry in the years ahead. This would not be merely a goal-setting and planning process but a discerning of God's call and leading into that future. Group three would explore the church of the present, building on this growing understanding of the church-as-a person. Group four would explore what would come to be called the inward journeying dimension of the life of faithfulness. Their goal would be to encourage individuals and groups to disciplines of quietness and prayer, and to provide resources and programs to support that effort. Words such as "mindfulness" and "attentiveness" dotted the report on their plans. Finally, group five would explore what would come to be called outward journeying, a focus on justice and social witness, a movement to counter what they had perceived as self-servingness and isolation in the church's current life and ministry. They observed that intimacy with God must be found "out there" in the clamor and neediness of the world, as well as in quietness and stillness within.

Though the phrase "sacred center" was not used at that time, this search for the heart and soul of Gladwyne Presbyterian Church made use of a replicable or adaptable process for congregations who want to recover their sacred center. We were discovering that what is true for individual Christians as they seek to ground their lives in the sacred center is true for the congregation, the church-as-a-person.

## Exploring the Church's History

The first task force designed a number of strategies to unearth and examine the church's hundred-plus years of history in their village. They tape-recorded interviews with the oldest and longest-standing members, inviting curious newer and younger members to listen in. A subgroup of the task force created a time line from a roll of craft paper that extended nearly seventy-five feet around three walls in the community room. Vertical lines, evenly spaced, marked the nine decades since the turn of the century, enough to span firsthand memory of all living members. Lines running laterally created three horizontal sections, the top captioned "in the world"; the middle, "in the church"; and the bottom, "in my life." Members were invited to write memories and perspectives, creating a running commentary on global, national, congregational, and personal history spanning nearly a century. Another panel of paper was posted on the fourth wall, prompted by the comments of a ninety-two-year-old in the church who said, "My grandfather used to hold me on his lap when I was five and tell me stories of *his* grandfather, when he first came to this church after the Civil War." We suddenly realized that we were only once removed, through the early memories of the oldest among us, from a century and a half of history, thus from all of this church's 110 years! Someone captioned that extra panel "the old, OLD stories."

Still another subgroup dubbed itself "Gladwyne archaeologists." Members rummaged through the church attic, collected boxes of stuff from informal, self-appointed church archivists, and found out who were the pack rats among the members. They found someone who had kept every church newsletter and bulletin for fifty-five years. They unearthed a growing collection of artifacts: creased and fading photographs, yellowed documents, and dust-covered minute books. They announced a plan to set up tables in the social room, inviting members to bring their memorabilia and artifacts. Older members took newer members on guided tours among the tables. To the older members' delight, newcomers were eager to hear these stories. It only took a glance at a torn and tattered old hymnbook, a tarnished communion chalice, or a hymnal rack salvaged from an old pew discarded in a sanctuary renovation to bring back long-forgotten or untold stories.

Over these months, an excitement about the church's history gained momentum. Older members felt an esteem they feared was lost. Younger members discovered a desire to share a history and heritage they never knew their church had.

The task force slowly became aware that it was doing more than merely collecting stories, artifacts, and memorabilia. Items drawn from endless basements and pulled from countless boxes were forming a rich tapestry. Spread across a century-plus, with a cast of thousands and no single artisan—what seemed at first glance to be only disconnected anecdotes—began to take on form and meaning.

With threads of shared belief and common purpose spanning generations, traditions, reconnected with their genesis, took on refreshed meaning. Delving into the formative and defining moments that gave rise to principles and practices valued for decades gave them new vitality and importance. And the church as a whole seemed to take on a personality and character peculiar to itself. Some sense of unique identity of the church came into clearer focus. We were not perfect; we never were. But by telling our story we became prouder of our church and more committed to writing its next chapters.

One member of the committee, a woman with a gift for succinctness, summarized its work with the following list of good reasons for any congregation to tell its stories and listen to its history. She realized that as we looked toward our past, we were at the same time looking toward our future. We looked to our history to

- claim its gifts
- learn its lessons
- heal its wounds
- identify its implicit values
- strengthen its roots and bonds
- honor its living saints
- unmask its secrets
- stabilize a launching pad for the future
- discern its trajectory toward the future
- freshen the wellsprings of the Spirit
- renew, perhaps rewriting its story

## Exploring the Church's Future

The second task force decided that the weeks following Epiphany, at the beginning of a new year, would be the appropriate time to invite the congregation to explore its future. A comment of one task force member, offered rather casually as the group convened, came to give focus and direction to its efforts. Recalling the biblical reflection at the fall retreat on the letters to the seven churches in Revelation and remembering that they were in search of the "angel of the church," this woman pointed out that angels do not decide what they want to do, but they hear and obey what God wants them to do. It is not so much that we decide about the future, as we discern God's future for this church.

The group decided to convene an all-day retreat the Saturday before the first Sunday in Epiphany, opening the day to the entire congregation but particularly urging church officers to attend. Nearly fifty people gathered in the living room of a nearby Catholic retreat center. A member of the task force began the day with what was intended to be a simple exercise, but it inspired personal reflection and dialogue that carried through the day. Each participant was given a sheet of paper with the story of the Wise Men printed on one side. On the other side were three questions, spaced so people had room to respond:

1. Name the people, circumstances, and things that guided the Wise Men's journey to Christ.
2. Name the people, circumstances, and things that have guided your journey to Christ.
3. Name the people, circumstances, and things that have guided our congregation's journey to Christ.

The group was amazed to discover that, though no one person listed more than six items, there were eighteen items on their collective list in response to the first question. Parishioners noted that some steps on the Wise Men's journey could have been carefully plotted and planned, while others would have unfolded as they traveled. The Magi departed without clarity or assurance about either destination or route. Trust was a cornerstone of their story.

Sharing in response to the second question was more intimate. People appreciated the open-endedness of the question. Most worksheets were crowded with words and phrases. Several insights surfaced. The vast majority of these events, they concluded, were not planned; they "just happened," it seemed, having a "life of their own." Though of no obvious or literal connection, clusters of events worked together to make a significant impact. In many cases it was recognized that the people named had not been aware of having played an important role in someone else's life. And many realized that only now, invited by this exercise, were they aware of how many people, circumstances, and things had guided their life journey.

But three observations stood out. First, this exercise had opened an awareness of an enhanced sense of meaning in life. It seemed as if some subtle and invisible hand, some meaning-giver had been at work. God's presence and involvement in life, the majority concluded, seemed more real, more specific and concrete. Second, certain discernment principles seemed implicit in these observations. Meaning in life, they concluded, was something to be noticed, welcomed, and embraced more than created or planned, more truly discerned than decided, more a matter of watchfulness and mindfulness. The group began to name discernment practices they might employ. Third, this exercise suggested the need for fresh approaches to plan the future.

The energy and momentum generated by the first two questions led to an enthusiastic discussion of the third. Building on the history-sharing work of the first task force, a spirit of rejoicing and celebration accompanied the process of discerning how God had guided the church's journey through its years.

Discernment, still a new idea to many, was beginning to be recognized as something vital to a truly faith-based planning process. The task force expanded its number to include a leader from a nearby Quaker community and a Roman Catholic sister, which led in turn to two open meetings on the practice of corporate discernment, then a series of neighborhood meetings to which the entire membership was invited in groups of twelve to fifteen. A common agenda was developed so that data from the meetings could be gathered in a useful way. Leaders were trained to facilitate the meetings. The letter to the congregation included this paragraph:

> In recent years our church has grown in many ways. One of those ways is becoming more attentive to our spiritual journeys—as individuals and as a church community. We have made a conscious decision to try to discover how and where God has been working in the history of our church, and where God may be leading and calling us now. We can only do this if the insight and vision of each of us is included. Small neighborhood groups are

being formed where we can share our spiritual journeys, pray and study scripture, and explore together how and where we sense God is seeking to lead us.[1]

I am convinced that something very basic in the mind-set of the church shifted at that retreat, shaping very new and different planning practices. One member suggested that, two decades before, the church had thrown open its doors to the brightest and best of management technology. Goal setting, action planning, management by objectives, participatory leadership, strategic decision making—methodology direct from the nation's most prestigious business schools—had captured the planning agenda of churches and judicatories. These resources were vital and valuable but, largely unnoticed, a worldview uninformed by biblical principles and Christian values had permeated congregational planning processes. Now the church realized discernment must precede decision making.

## Exploring the Church in the Present

This group designed its work to take place over several months. Members asked me to preach a sermon on the "angel of the church," then made printed copies available. A newsletter article further interpreted the theme, encouraging members to read that sermon and welcome the ongoing work of their task force. They took "fanning out" and "creative infiltrating" very seriously.

Members of the task force asked for time on the agenda of every church board, committee, and study group. They visited women's circles and men's breakfasts; they came to Sunday school classes and invited themselves to house church groups; they ate pizza with the youth group and sipped tea with the senior citizens. And they asked countless individual members a series of simple questions. Asking people to image the church-as-a person, an idea that began to garner increased understanding and evoke increasing curiosity, they asked: (1) What are the strengths of our church-as-a-person? What features of our church make you proud? What are its endearing and engaging characteristics? What is most appealing about its personality? What is it good at? (2) What are the weaknesses of our church-as-a-person? What makes you less than proud of it? What is annoying and off-putting about it? What traits would you want to change? (3) What do you think must happen for the church to change? The interviewers insisted that this effort could be helpful only if everyone was thoroughly honest.

They began to hear phrases repeated. "This church is welcoming and friendly, . . . cozy and comfortable, . . . inclusive and nonjudgmental, . . . open-minded and innovative." Appreciation usually came first. "Gladwyne Church is gregarious, . . . attractive, . . . rather young, . . . in good physical shape." "It is intellectual but likes to express its feelings." More neutral observations and criticisms came next. "This church is affluent and snobbish, . . . suburban and suburbanized, . . . affluent, elite, and awfully white." "It is remote and removed, isolated and insulated." "It is charitable, but not much concerned for justice." "It can be stuffy." The criticisms were harder to voice and to hear. But as defenses lowered, honest criticism seemed creative and positive, even when the words seemed harsh. Such candor felt strangely refreshing. Some masks were falling away. We felt more noble and courageous.

People got curious about how the church as a person got this way—how it developed both its positive and negative characteristics. As is true of a person, we realized these traits took a long time to form and would likely be painful to change. But we found ourselves emboldened. As directed in the fourth recovery step in Alcoholics Anonymous, we had conducted a "fearless moral inventory," and as in step five, we had shared it with another. We were facing honestly who we were. We were beginning to release energy to become who we might be. False self was beginning to yield to truer or higher self.

## Exploring the Inward Journey

Like Jesus' disciples, the congregation at large seemed to be asking, "Lord, teach us to pray." A task force member who had just finished reading a less than helpful book on Christian devotion said, "I feel like an expert on prayer, but I still don't know how to pray!" This task force decided to encourage this broadening desire to learn to pray, then to provide resources to meet that desire. A one-year commitment to use the New Common Lectionary was well received. I wrote a daily devotional guide called "The Daily Walk." To support a growing interest in contemplative spirituality in the

church, these monthly booklets offered a decidedly monastic approach. Each day offered an "entrance meditation," a quiet invitation to inwardness, a time of silence and stillness, then a paragraph
of introduction to a biblical text—the Old Testament, psalm, epistle,
and Gospel readings in turn. Church school curriculum, which had
been created by the teaching teams for several years, was based on
the lectionary lessons, and I preached each week from those texts.

The task force offered a series of half-day Saturday retreats each
month on such themes as quieting our minds and hearts; listening
to life and keeping a journal; understanding how to study the Bible;
learning to pray; pondering our dreams; relating prayer to work,
parenting, friendship building, and social life. Three members of
the church who had received special training in spiritual guidance
made themselves available as spiritual friends to assist those desiring a deeper prayer life. Guidelines were prepared to conduct the
business of church meetings more prayerfully. This task force
suggested to the church board that there be sabbath weeks spaced
through the year, during which all church programs and meetings,
except worship and Sunday school, would be suspended for seven
days.

The task force wanted to nurture ever-deepening individual
commitment to Bible study and prayer, hoping this would
strengthen a spirit of community, but their interest went even farther
than that. In the first few months after the fall retreat, the image of
"angel of the church" seemed little more than an abstract idea. But
then almost imperceptibly a spirit of oneness began forming. Someone once said that the word *koinonia*, the biblical word for both
"community" and "sharing," means more than people lovingly
approaching each other, more than profoundly touching one another. Rather it suggests lives overlapping, intermingling, in some
ultimate and mystical communion. We had not coined the phrase
yet, but in retrospect I call it "sacred center."

## Exploring the Outward Journey

The work of this fifth task force proved to be the easiest. Rather
than impose a new process on the congregation, they decided to
join the momentum of an already rapidly expanding mission and
outreach ministry at the church. This was early in the Reagan

administration, and what would become major cutbacks in publicly funded social welfare programs were already underway. President Reagan visited Philadelphia in the spring of 1982 and challenged church leaders at a breakfast meeting to take up the slack from these cutbacks. A church board member, with calculator in hand, pointed out that Philadelphia-area congregations would have to raise an average of $98,000 per church to meet that challenge. He loved to tease the largely Republican congregation with that figure.

Remembering a theme Walter Wink had raised at the weekend retreat the prior September, the task force identified a unique contribution they could make to this overall outward-journey mandate. "Faithfulness must move us beyond charity to justice," someone remembered Walter saying. He had talked about a call to faithfulness to "thrones, dominions, principalities, and powers"— the structures of government—as well as to individuals.

Guided by materials from Bread for the World, the task force began to challenge the congregation to become knowledgeable about public policy, pending legislation, and governmental process as it related to the poor, and to find ways to affect this decision-making process. They set up literature tables in the back of the sanctuary, encouraged members to write letters to legislators, and led a contingent of church members to the federal building in the center city to protest some of the budget cutbacks. A new dimension was added to the basic definition of outward journeying at the church.

This is one congregation's approach to deepening congregational self-understanding. This particular effort stretched across eighteen months a decade and a half ago, but its impact continues in the life of the church today. The church became more than *like* a person. It became in a very real way a trusted friend, a colleague, a companion. Just as the church was a sacred place that invited us to explore the depths leading toward our sacred centers, we in turn had glimpsed something of its sacred center.

*Chapter Eight*

# Rising to the Challenge
## Reflections on Leadership

Churches need leaders who can rise to a formidable challenge, laced with danger and rich with opportunity, leaders who are self-transcending and self-motivated, inspired and inspiring. Such leaders are grounded in the best of tradition, yet discern and then embody fresh vision for the future. They are of deep rooting and clear personhood, flexible, resilient, and innovative. They blend character and competence. They have strong personal presence, gracefulness and balance, and a sense of authority. They are called to artfulness and hard work.

New leaders must blend assertiveness and receptivity, firmness and flexibility, certainty and openmindedness. These new leaders must have growing self-awareness, a commitment to personal and professional development, an openness to feedback, and an attentiveness to self-care. These leaders are ready to be assertive yet collaborative and comfortable with partnership as well. Such qualities, including those explored in this chapter, emerge from a commitment to recover the sacred center.

A poster hangs inside my office closet door, so I catch a glimpse of it regularly. Its caption reads, "Be patient, God isn't finished with me yet." Your agenda for personal and leadership development may differ from the ones I propose here. But I urge you to see yourself as continually in process, deepening spiritually and becoming more competent. Commit to no less for yourself, and support no less in others.

## Spiritual Depth and Commitment

For the past eight years my wife and I have taught in a doctor of ministry program. The focus of our course is designing and leading marriage and family enrichment events in the local church setting. In the process of teaching I inevitably refer to my personal devotional life. Each year, once the setting feels safe, students will confess that they simply do not pray or read Scripture for themselves and that they are not sure they know how!

My colleague and friend Chuck Olsen conducted over two hundred exit interviews with church officers from several denominations as they completed a term of service. Over 50 percent of these leaders said they were "less than satisfied" with the experience, while 20 percent said they were significantly disappointed, even disillusioned. There was remarkable consistency in the reasons they offered. "I didn't know at the beginning, and I never really did figure out, just what I was supposed to do," was a common response. "I couldn't see much of a difference, really, between working on the church board and working in other organizations, or even going to work," was another typical comment. Uniformly, people found the meetings to be dull, long, lifeless, and without discernible spiritual grounding.

The most troubling finding in this research was almost unanimous agreement on the single greatest disappointment. "I agreed to serve on the board as a way to continue and deepen my spiritual development," a typical respondent would say, "but in the course of serving, my spiritual life was interrupted. No, it was impeded, detoured, virtually halted, maybe even reversed."

Many church members have a growing longing for a richer and more disciplined spiritual life. Protestants show a growing interest in what Roman Catholics call "spiritual formation." Chuck Olsen's work invites churches and their members to envision terms of service on church boards, including meetings and the concrete work of service as spiritual formation.[1]

A growing number of excellent books nurture personal spiritual development in very practical ways. At least two Protestant and numerous Roman Catholic institutions offer certification to spiritual directors who are now widely available to those seeking a spiritual mentor.[2]

Pastors and lay leaders who are going to inspire in others and their congregations a commitment to inward journeying, individual and congregational discernment, to reinventing the church—to recovering the sacred center—will themselves need to be people of spiritual depth and commitment.

## A Journey of Psychological Healing

One of John Denver's songs begins, "I was born in the summer of my twenty-seventh year." Well, I was born in the fall of my twenty-eighth year. At an encounter group, after fourteen years of personal slumbering, of unconsciousness, I woke up and began to take responsibility for my life. My journey of psychological healing began that week. It became, I continue to discover, a lifetime adventure.

After my mother died when I was fourteen, as a result of apparently routine surgery, the support and love of my pastor and church community stirred in me a first sense of call to local church ministry. I spoke of these things earlier, but there is more to the story. The afternoon and evening of the day she died I cried for hours. I cried through dinner. I cried with the arrival of each person at the front door. I cried myself to sleep. Then I stopped crying—for fourteen years! Paul Simon sang of it: "I touch no one and no one touches me. I am a rock, I am an island." The psychic doors slammed shut.

My call to ministry, I recognize in retrospect, had another dimension. Becoming a minister, my unconscious concluded, would provide a role, a source of affirmation, for me. Becoming ordained offered a persona, a "self" with which to meet the world, a mask to hide behind. All of this helped to hold my life together, giving me clarity, meaning, purpose—and a vocation. I had a title and built-in status. Seminary training colluded in the development of my mask, I think, by telling me who I was, how I was to dress, and how I was to behave. All was neatly and comfortably in place. I had, of course, no awareness of any of this. In fact, if it was to work, it was necessary that it remain completely unconscious.

As a consequence, tragically, all relationships in my life, including those with my wife and children, were formed through the lens of this incomplete, significantly contrived and unreal self.

My healing began with an impish Japanese minister and human relations trainer named Arnold Nakajima. Arnie was leading a five-day group process in which I was a participant. He saw through my mask immediately! He told me at the end of the five days that he made a decision at the outset that whenever he looked at me or spoke to me, he would address only the lonely, frightened child he sensed inside of me. I hastened to bar the door and ward off what I could see only as danger. But Arnie was lovingly persistent. Little more than glimpses of light and love penetrated my shell that week. The walls were not breached, but some cracks formed. The process had begun.

In the decades since, I have added chapters to my story. I was graced by the power of healing prayer. New levels of intimacy became possible. I became steadily more open and trusting, transparent and alive. I had to muster the courage to reevaluate my call to ministry. Happily, in the process my sense of vocation took on fresh rooting and renewed vitality.

This work of healing—the psychological dimension of recovering the sacred center—is, I believe, a responsibility as well as a profound privilege for those who choose to become leaders in search of the reinvented future church. This is only a glimpse at my story. The healing story that truly counts is your own.

## Balance and Presence

My life as a pastor is full of important tasks, or so I like to convince myself. I have an "important file" that contains lists of the truly urgent things. Some years ago I arrived at my office on a Monday morning in early September, a month in the church year when the "important things" seem particularly important. The "important file" was gone! I panicked! I looked everywhere. I rummaged frantically through each pile of papers scattered around my office. I checked the trash can, unemptied since Friday. No luck. I asked the church secretary. It was gone!

I did not find it later that week or even later that month. It was, it seemed, truly gone. To make matters worse, I had little memory of just what the file contained. Then, six months later, I found it! I have one of those old desks with a shelf that slides out to hold papers. Under the shelf is a skinny drawer that is rather useless if you regularly use the shelf, so I did not keep anything in that drawer. During a March clean-up, I opened the drawer. There was the file folder!

I eagerly opened it. It contained fifteen "important things to do." I had completed only seven or perhaps eight of them. Half were left undone. The greater embarrassment was to admit that, as much as I could discern, it had not made a particle of difference! So much for the importance of "important things"!

Those drawn to local church leadership, clergy and laity alike, seem particularly vulnerable to workaholism and burnout. Such leaders pay the price of undue fatigue and anxiety, diverting time and attention that rightfully belong to family and friends and betraying in the process faith in God's love. Educator and author Parker Palmer suggests that our overgiving, overfunctioning, and overworking unmask in us a "functional atheism."[3] New leaders of a renewed church are committed to balance, grace, and mindfulness, even as they serve with vigor and diligence.

## Tolerance for Uncertainty and Chaos

I would rather live in a Newtonian world. I like things in their place. I am drawn to predictability and control. I want to know the rules, and I want everyone to play by them. At the beginning of a given day or week, I would love to distribute three-by-five cards, giving each person with whom I will interact their lines and stage directions. I would write the script and they would play the parts. That is not a bad summary of how congregational leaders viewed and played their role not so many years ago.

Approaches to leadership that seek predictability and control simply do not work in today's world. Individuals and organizations operate with spontaneity and unpredictability. Effective leaders foster a tolerance for uncertainty, even chaos. This appropriate tolerance is hard to define, but clarity, firmness, and consistency must be woven with a willingness to be uncertain and incomplete.

Leaders of the reinvented church will have high tolerance for ambiguity and uncertainty. They must learn to see ambiguity as an invitation to a different, perhaps deeper, sense of order and meaning.

Creative leaders must even have a high tolerance for apparent chaos. Some years ago I attended a conference, a dialogue between systematic theologians from Princeton Seminary and physics professors from Princeton University. The theologians spoke in carefully constructed sentences and in even, measured tones. They appeared definite and quietly confident. They presented an orderly, logical, truly systematic worldview. Their words were reassuring to me. The physicists, however, searched for words, and with sweeping gestures that almost propelled them out of their chairs, spoke of a different world. Their words were filled with a sense of mystery and delight.

"There are no laws," suggested a physicist. "There are only probabilities. High probabilities. Dependabilities. Apparent certainties. But they remain only probabilities," he insisted. "That can't be," I silently argued.

"The molecules of a gas under pressure behave haphazardly and unpredictably," said another scientist. "Haphazardly? Unpredictably? That just can't be," I assured myself. These comments were most unsettling to me.

A third physicist delivered what seemed to be the crushing blow. "Light can be either particle action or wave action," he stated, rather matter-of-factly. "It seems to depend on what the viewer expects," he concluded.

"You mean that light 'chooses,' it 'decides' which to be, depending on what the viewer is thinking?" I asked, fearing the answer.

"Well, not quite. But you will see what you *expect* to see," he said. I was nonplussed. The theologians were silent.

Shortly before he published his basic theory of evolution, Charles Darwin had a lively exchange of letters with Aldous Huxley. Huxley challenged Darwin's insistence that evolution proceeded by "gradualism," a slow, steady upward trajectory. Darwin held a Western European bias for order and predictability. Stephen Jay Gould and Ilya Prigogine have more recently demonstrated that, as Huxley argued, evolution proceeds by what is called "punctuated equilibrium"—a movement from homeostasis, through "perturbation" or chaos, to reintegration.

These lessons from quantum physics and chaos theory have

application to organizations and congregations. These dynamics are at play in the evolution toward the reinvented future church. As physicist Prigogine suggests in his "theory of dissipative structures," seasons of stability and homeostasis must yield to seasons of chaos and apparent disintegration if they are ultimately to lead to seasons of reintegration at higher levels of form.[4] The new leader needs to be ready simply to "hold the center" in patience and trust as we move from what was to what is to be.

Leaders who develop a tolerance for ambiguity and even chaos will also develop a high tolerance for "deep ecumenism," as Matthew Fox calls it.[5] I served for two years as interim minister at Honey Brook Presbyterian Church. When my former presbytery received the request that I serve the congregation, they sent a formal statement discouraging this proposal. "Howard is much too liberal for Honey Brook," they insisted. "We do not recommend this arrangement." Honey Brook hired me anyway.

An argument can be made that I was "too liberal" for Honey Brook. We were an unlikely partnership, yet we chose to respect each other. We loved the Lord and explored the Scriptures together. We carried out the life and work of the congregation together. One Sunday at a coffee hour after church, a man who had disagreed with me about almost everything approached me, shook my hand, looked me squarely in the eye, and said, "Howard, we don't agree on much. We hold our faith in different ways and we talk about our faith in different words, but I trust you. In fact, I love you!"

I am a member of a denomination perhaps best known in recent years for its theological and ideological collisions. I am citizen of a nation whose political candidates, no matter the party or office, have raised sarcasm and disrespect to an art form. Given that context, I view my time at Honey Brook and my relationship with its people as a sign of hope. We spoke different languages. We named our truth using different words. We held substantially different opinions and points of view. But love built a bridge.

People everywhere are longing for an invitation and opportunity to ponder the deep things of life. They want to listen to their own truth, then to share it in words that are natural and authentic to them. Churches are often perceived as unwelcoming to that process. All too often they are!

# A Person of Authority

The Gladwyne Church officers gathered one October Saturday for an annual leadership retreat. Subgroups of four were exploring a question assigned by the leader for the day. I slipped out to make a phone call. I returned in a few moments through the kitchen. As I began to open the door to the meeting room, I hesitated for some reason. Mark's voice caught my ear. "I don't know why we're doing all this," he said firmly. "Howard's gonna do what he damn well pleases anyway." I stepped back and let the door close. I was stunned and hurt. I pondered my options and did not like any of them. Finally, I pushed through the door, walked to Mark's table, and whispered, "I want you to share what you said with the total group." He hesitated. I insisted. He shared the comment.

There was not overwhelming agreement with what Mark said, though most said there was more than a grain of truth in it. The facilitator for the meeting helped us to talk about how we had been working together. There was clearly a problem, we concurred, but it was not all my problem. Yes, I had been all too prone to exercise my influence in manipulative and autocratic ways. But if I had been "taking the bait," someone was "throwing the line." As a leadership team, we began to see the pattern we had established, and we decided we wanted to change it. We pledged to be candid with one another in a feedback process. We made a commitment to rework the leadership process and restructure the organizational plan in search of truer participation and empowerment.

At the heart of this incident was the issue of authority. How did I, an ordained minister and the head of staff of the church, view my authority? How did laypeople in leadership and in the congregation view my authority and their own? I am convinced that unresolved authority issues are a major source of congregational conflict, ineffectiveness, confusion, and malaise.

Congregational leaders, lay and clergy alike, have spoken the politically correct language of participation and empowerment for some years. Few have moved from lip service to enactment. And few will, until issues of authority are addressed and resolved.

## Called, Gifted, Purposeful, and Passionate

Jesus said that we could know a tree by its fruit. Healthy trees yield bountiful harvests. Joseph Campbell said, "Follow your bliss." A poet once said, "Your heart knows the way." Leadership emerges from the inside out, with a recovering of the sacred center.

I awoke at 1:30 A.M. I slipped out of bed, groped for my journal in the dark, and made my way to the den. I knew my thoughts would keep me awake until I gave them some attention. I wrote just one sentence at first, which seemed to flow on its own. "It's time," I wrote. Only that, "It's time." I could not pretend that I did not know what it meant. That two-word sentence announced to me that it was time to complete my work at Gladwyne Church. I wrote barely a full page, offering no reasons. There was only a simple clarity. Knowing that I might resist this truth in the morning, I dated and signed the bottom of the sheet.

There was no logic to that decision. My colleagues, when I told them, thought I had lost my senses. The congregation was persistent and persuasive as it worked to change my mind. My wife, Betsy, was hurt and sad, and asked that I reconsider or wait a year. I tried to honor her request but only found myself increasingly clear and unwavering. She asked me why, but the answers I ventured seemed hollow and contrived. Finally, I responded in the language that had become central to our basic understanding of Christian faithfulness at Gladwyne Church. My calling, the focus of my gifts for ministry, my clarity of purpose, and most important, my passion had begun to ebb. The work we were doing together at Gladwyne Church continued to appear important. The mission of the congregation seemed no less clear to me. The road ahead remained exciting, and the invitation to travel it compelling. But my discernment of call, gift, purpose, and passion was in transition. I did not know what was next, but I did know it was time to begin completing my work with that community.

The grieving process was not easy. Joy mingled with pain our last Sunday, after twenty-three years of ministry. Yet I knew I had acted in alignment with a basic value and principle that the Gladwyne community and I shared—to find faithfulness in life and ministry through discerning *call, gift, purpose, and passion*.

The new leader, venturing toward the reinvented church, will act out of a similar inner clarity and rootedness. No single commitment was more clarifying and empowering for ministry at Gladwyne Church than this fourfold understanding of the rhythm of personal and congregational faithfulness—listening for the inner call, stirring the gifts for ministry that reside within, inviting clarity of purpose, and welcoming the fires of inner passion for ministry and service.

## Continual Growth and Learning

Not many years ago people would complete the learning phase of life by their early twenties, then pursue their career. Education, then application. People learned their trade or got their degree and then began their work. The technology of a given field, even a complex and complicated one, would go largely unchanged for decades. This is no longer true for anyone today, including congregational leaders.

Continual learning is necessary if one is to be an effective leader of a vital congregation. Today continual learning is recognized to be natural, satisfying a basic human desire to grow and contribute. The new leader will learn by experience as well as learning from specific educational opportunities. People and organizations will find a balance of individual and team learning.

A middle manager in a large manufacturing corporation spoke up emphatically at a recent church board retreat. He told us that no one would ever be promoted to a new position in his company, with new kinds of management and leadership responsibility, without intense and highly focused training. He persuasively pointed out that the chair of their Christian education committee was an insurance salesman, the chair of the stewardship committee a shopkeeper, and the chair of the worship committee a high school teacher—all serving in their respective roles with limited effectiveness, he thought, because they had had no training, not even a basic briefing. I helped the board develop a continuing education curriculum for church leaders at all levels of responsibility in the congregation and invited them to take advantage of training opportunities offered by their judicatory.

In this pilgrimage toward the reinvented future church, each leader and each congregation will seek to make contributions to the art of leadership and congregational development. Churches will become lay academies, on-site seminaries, communities of people committed to building character and competence.

## A Congruent and Faithful Lifestyle

In July 1986, my wife and I accompanied a youth group from Gladwyne Church on a ten-day mission trip to Port au Prince, Haiti, the poorest country in the Western hemisphere. We walked the narrow passageways of Cité Soleil, which Mother Teresa said is the poorest neighborhood on the face of the planet. We rocked babies with AIDS to sleep. We dressed the wounds of people for whom a cut on their foot, through infection, would ultimately be fatal. Our hearts broke.

In August, just a month later, back from Haiti and on a family summer vacation, we walked along the docks of a marina at Montauk Point, New York, awed by the sleek and shimmering elegance of yachts in their slips. We returned later that evening to our modest summer cottage. After our ten days in Haiti, however, nothing seemed modest! Something in our lives had to change. We began what we have come to call our family commitment to "downward mobility." A year later we made a family decision to sell that "modest summer cottage" and distribute the $80,000 proceeds to do grassroots work among the poor. We continue to wrestle with our personal commitment to economic justice. Our current struggle is how to embody justice in dealing with what we anticipate receiving as inheritance from our parents and how to structure our wills.

My wife and I have come to believe that personal faithfulness and the call to leadership compel us to ongoing, hands-on, side-by-side work in partnership with the poor. We have much to learn about our lingering racism, do-goodism, and paternalism. We seek to move beyond idealizing the poor into a truer, deeper solidarity. This commitment has led us to the homeless on the streets of Philadelphia, to the eastside section of Chester, and perhaps shortly to the mushroom farms of Chester County.

To name lifestyle issues as essential to becoming a faithful and effective leader risks sounding arbitrary and arrogant, biased perhaps by only our experience and value system. "Holier than thou" may even come to mind. Nevertheless, I offer this for your reflection.

*Chapter Nine*

# Claiming
# Congregational Potential
## Moving from Possibility to Reality

My two sons, ages nine and eleven at the time, arrived at the dinner table one evening with strange and gleeful smiles on their faces. David, the older of the two, held something in his hand, which he slipped under his chair as he sat down. My curiosity was piqued, but I resisted the temptation to ask. Instead of their usual "'scuse me" and hasty departure when we were finished, they remained, uncharacteristically, at the table. Finally, David reached under his chair and ceremoniously dropped at my place a stack of old and yellowed documents, card stock paper folded in half.

"My report cards!" I exclaimed. The boys had been cleaning the attic to make a club house for their friends, and had been rummaging through my memorabilia. Ironically, just a few nights earlier I had made my sons sit at this same dining room table while I gave them a pep talk about working harder in school, doing a better job on their homework, and having, in general, a better attitude about their education.

Their find gave them much to talk about! My grades, they had noticed, were strictly mediocre, but that was not the worst of it. They were quick to point out that I had an unbroken string of U's (for "unsatisfactory") in classroom behavior from grades one through five. Eric, the shyer of the two, spoke up, with obvious delight: "Every grade period your teachers wrote, 'Howard is not living up to his potential.'"

As we continued the conversation, I found myself transported back to those elementary school classrooms, bringing to mind almost every teacher and seeing the scenes that earned me those mediocre grades and less than appreciative comments. I paused in my remembering in my sixth grade classroom. Mrs. Hutt was the teacher, my streak of U's was broken, my grades improved, and her comments were positive. I began to blossom as a student and to relate better with my peers and the teachers. I started to "live up to my potential." What had Mrs. Hutt done to awaken the potential in me?

Seven years later, my wife and I were sitting with David, then eighteen and a high school senior, and his high school advisor, Mr. McGovern, for a final evaluation and to review his plans for the future. David had survived a long struggle with learning disabilities and the emotional stress they create to become a steady B- student in the academic track of the high school curriculum. The advisor leaned forward, cupped his chin on his open hands, looked first at me, then at Betsy, and said, "I hope you are proud of your son. I hope you realize what a hard-working, diligent, and courageous student he has been. He has performed beyond his potential. I hope you're as proud of him as I am."

I found myself wondering just what had turned things around for David. After years of being a hesitant, shy, often frustrated grade school student, he had suddenly become a self-assured, capable, and rather contented high school student. I looked up to find my answer. It was Mr. McGovern, his high school advisor. I asked the same question I had asked about Mrs. Hutt: What had Tom McGovern done to awaken the potential in David?

This question was recently and even more poignantly raised when I officiated at a memorial service for Chuck, a friend of a parishioner, just a day before what would have been his fifty-sixth birthday. Chuck had graduated at the top of his law school class, became a highly successful attorney, and was attractive, outgoing, athletic, and well liked. Everything was going Chuck's way until March 17, 1978, the day he had three heart attacks in less than five minutes, complicated by anoxia, a deprivation of oxygen to the brain. He hovered near death for several weeks.

Chuck survived. Two of his friends remember seeing him the first day he was allowed visitors. "There he was," Jock remembers, "tall, muscular, attractive. 'Same old Chuck,' I thought to myself, as I approached him down the hallway. Then I saw him up close. His eyes looked empty, and he obviously didn't have any idea who I was. I left wondering if I'd ever see the 'old Chuck' again," he concluded. Chuck's IQ, which had been nearly 150, was now computed at 67.

Linn, the second friend, lingered to talk with the doctor. "Linn," the doctor began to explain, "Chuck hasn't lost anything, really. Nothing has gone away. Everything Chuck ever knew, his ability to think and feel, his knowledge of the law, all his memories, are still there, inside. Will they come back out? I can't answer that. They may, and they may not. But I can say this," he went on: "They can't be forced out. They can't be commanded out. No one can make them come out. They'll have to be encouraged out, coaxed out, drawn out by patience."

Linn made a decision that day and encouraged a circle of friends to join him. He decided that if encouragement, patience, faithfulness, and love were needed to bring Chuck back, it would come from them.

Those who gathered after Chuck's memorial service were able to celebrate how much did come back, how much of what had retreated deep inside Chuck amid the trauma of his heart attacks and anoxia had returned. I stood to one side and asked myself the question I had asked about Mrs. Hutt and Tom McGovern: What had Linn and his friends done to awaken the potential in Chuck?

## Actualizing Potential in People and Congregations

I suggested in chapter 7 that a church is like a person, that we can understand a congregation's life and behavior as we would that of an individual. Like David, Chuck, and me, congregations have potential—for creativity, productivity, and relationship. Like David, Chuck, and me, they may or may not have and realize that potential. Congregations need a Mrs. Hutt, a Tom McGovern, a Linn and his friends to see that potential and call it out. This is part of what congregational leadership is all about.

What happens when a person actualizes his or her potential, when inner possibility becomes outward reality? Is there some logical process involved in reaching potential? If so, can we promote greater realization of potential? Acknowledging that the process is subtle, I suggest five stages in the process of realizing potential. These apply to both individuals and organizations.

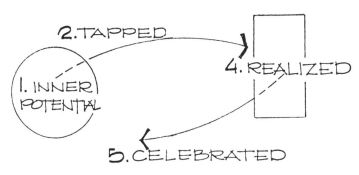

## 1. Potential as Entitlement

Self-realization begins with a sense of entitlement, a deep and hearty belief that an inner potential exists in the first place. No one can escape damage to self-confidence. The struggle with self-esteem seems universal, but realization of potential begins with naming and celebrating it.

Mrs. Hutt created an atmosphere in her classroom and had a regard for her students that helped me to name and believe in my potential. Mr. McGovern joked with David, prodded him, looked him square in the eye, until David began to trust this affirmation. David began to stand taller, walk more boldly, talk more forcibly, and look others in the eye. He began to believe in himself. Linn and his friends visited Chuck regularly, related persistently to the "Chuck within," even when the outer Chuck remained expressionless and unresponsive. Their commitment was sustained over months and years.

Some deep inner longing and stirring, muted but not silenced, assaulted but not vanquished, gives rise to a sense of entitlement, and potentiality is born or reborn. Mrs. Hutt, Tom McGovern, Linn and Jock did not create the potential, but they released it. They discovered it, then invited David, Chuck, and me to rediscover it and believe in it, and then to manifest it. Recovering the sacred center gives rise to the celebration of an inner self of extraordinary possibility and potential, a birthright at the heart of creation and the created.

## 2. Tapping the Potential

Awareness of inner potential becomes animated by the permission, encouragement, and empowerment to mobilize that potential. Seeing coals in the hearth, we blow the sparks into flame. This step, like the others, demands initiative and courage.

My friend Aaron refinishes furniture. We sat one day in his basement shop as he worked patiently on a drawer front of a small chest, a rather unattractive piece, I thought to myself. A thick coat of blue paint broke away in chunks as he carefully worked with a special scraping tool. A coat of faded yellow peeked out from beneath. "Got a ways to go, I'd guess," Aaron said quietly. Sure enough, the first chips of yellow revealed a blue-green layer beneath. Aaron deftly worked his blade without missing a beat in our conversation. I think he did mutter a bit when the first blue-green paint chipped away to reveal dark brown. An hour later the first peak of natural wood peered through, and only days later, after endless careful strokes of the blade, was all the paint removed. And only weeks later was the refinishing job complete. Potential I had not even glimpsed had been seen, then claimed by Aaron's patience and craftsmanship.

After first believing in a rich and vibrant inner potential—of person or congregation—we must then mobilize that potential. Possibility starts its journey toward actuality. Steps one and two occur within the person or congregation. They are the fruit of inner work and become the essential raw material of faithfulness and effectiveness in the outer world.

## 3. Directing the Potential

A hearth contains fire in order to generate heat and light. An engine contains exploding gasoline to fire the pistons and power the drive train. Raw, unbridled energy of inner potential, once tapped, must be focused and directed.

I never liked the third beatitude, "Blessed are the meek, for they shall inherit the earth." I always heard it as, "Blessed are the doormats, the jellyfish, the pushovers, the wimps." Then someone told me that the Greek word for "meek" comes from the same root as the word for "bridling a wild animal so it can be ridden or yoked for work" or "harnessing a wild river to turn a mill or irrigate a field." So mobilized personal potential must become "meek." Named and claimed personal potential must be aimed in the service of accomplishing goals and expressing creativity.

Remember when Alice and her companion arrived breathlessly at a fork in a road somewhere in Wonderland? They were in an obvious rush. The Red Queen stood in typical elegance at the fork. "Which way should we go?" asked Alice with urgency in her voice.

"Well, where do you want to go?" the Red Queen replied.

"I don't know," Alice muttered.

"Then, I suppose," the Red Queen answered, "it doesn't make much difference which road you take!"

Many people and congregations, having tapped potential and energy, fail to give it focus and direction. They become unfocused and fragmented. Getting direction means clarifying vision, defining measurable, manageable, and time-targeted goals, forging clear and concise objectives, working a strategic plan, then carrying it all out.

## 4. Realizing the Potential

Self-defeating patterns can intrude at every step through this process. For many *wanting* and *reaching* are nullified by an unwillingness or inability to *take*. Entitlement can collapse just short of the point of fulfillment. To alter the words of Jesus, "Ask, but do not receive; knock, but do not open; seek, but do not find." The capacity to persevere and accomplish is often thwarted. Many come to the very edge of fulfillment, to the brink of achieving their goal, only to shrink away. Those who fully actualize their potential take that next step. For many the first step feels more like a leap.

I will not forget the last moments of the 1988 Olympic Games. Less festive and orchestrated than more recent closings, the cameras were fixed on a simple stage and a rather undramatic though touching ceremony. In the midst of someone's speech a camera panned to the spot where the marathon track entered the stadium. Long after the last runners had crossed the finish line, a lone figure arrived, running at a pained but steady gait, until he too crossed the finish line. There was something touching in his dogged

determination to complete the race. Claiming personal and congregational potential is a long-distance run, not a sprint. Indeed, at
times it makes the demands of a marathon.

## 5. Celebrating Potential's Fulfillment

This circle of actualizing potential is completed when there is
delight and rejoicing in the process and its fruit. We will speak later
about the importance of celebrating faithfulness, not just success.
Not all effort can be fruitful, but it can be honest and faithful. The
members of a Bible study group, noting Peter's "failure" to sustain
his walk on the water, decided to compile a "St. Peter scoreboard."
After collaborative research they discovered that there are eleven
occasions in the Gospels where Peter sought to respond to Jesus
faithfully. He was successful on four occasions and failed in the
other seven. "He didn't even bat .500," someone commented.

"Wait a minute," a man who loved baseball interrupted. "If you
bat .300 in baseball, you'll likely make five million bucks a year
and go to the Hall of Fame. But for every three times you go to the
plate and end up on base, you walk back to the dugout seven times.
Guess we should get to the plate as much as we can!"

## Applying This Process

Gary had served the four-hundred-plus-member congregation,
Centerville Presbyterian Church, for eight years. Gary was called
by the congregation to be its pastor with a broad consensus that he
was the "right person at the right time" for the church. In ways that
some at the church saw as a replay of a still earlier pastor's
departure, Gary's predecessor had left in the midst of conflict and
controversy. Gary was quiet, likeable, and understated. Soon after
his arrival the waters, which had been deeply troubled, quieted, and
the lines of hostility that had been firmly drawn faded. The air at
the church cleared, and the atmosphere became noticeably more
peaceful. Everyone seemed relieved.

Charlotte had become the associate minister three years before
Gary's arrival. She had served through that era of controversy
surrounding the previous senior minister, which had etched a certain caution into her spirit. She was quick to wonder out loud
whether some residue of that era lingered beneath the apparent

calm, and whether some wounds from that time, now a decade ago, remained unhealed.

Two issues had recently stirred conflict in the congregation, motivating Gary and Charlotte to call me at the Parish Empowerment Network. The first revolved around the possibility of replacing the hymnbooks at the church. The Presbyterian Church had recently published a new hymnbook that included contemporary hymns and praise songs, as well as hymns drawn from other cultures and languages. This new hymnbook also deleted some hymns from the previous edition, hymns many older church members view as old favorites. The editors also altered the wording of some hymns in an attempt to make the language more inclusive.

The worship committee, with the support of Gary and Charlotte, proposed to the board that the church purchase new hymnbooks, using memorial fund reserves. The board, wanting to move cautiously, chose to announce to the congregation that it was exploring the possibility of purchasing new hymnbooks. Board members made it clear that no decision had been made, nor was a decision imminent. Nevertheless, ripples of disgruntlement widened across the congregation. Gary was surprised. Charlotte wondered if she was seeing the same old sides forming, just like a decade ago.

The second issue revolved around the desire of a group of young adults, under the leadership of Charlotte, to form a Christian yoga class. The controversy that ensued in the congregation did not seem to follow a predictable pattern. Those who expressed opposition were those Charlotte called the middle adults, those who had joined the church five to twelve years ago. These people complained that this program was "new age," as they called it. The sponsoring group of young adults said they would be glad to form the group only for themselves and not publicize it in the Sunday bulletin or the monthly newsletter. The opposition only stiffened.

I met Gary and Charlotte with two members of the board for a breakfast meeting. Each of the four contributed as they offered an updated commentary on the events of recent months, observing that the congregation seemed immobilized by the controversy surrounding these two issues. As they were speaking, I found myself doodling on the back of an extra paper place mat. That scribbling would ultimately become the finished drawing on page 128. All of the elements in that completed graphic seemed to be present in their congregational dynamics.

First, I drew a circle, captioned CONGREGATIONAL POTEN-TIAL. I retraced the circle four or five times, as if to suggest energy and centrifugal force. Then I instructed the group to picture the congregation as an aggregate of potential energy, the merged collective energy of the members of the church, symbolized by this circle. This energy is both collective and synergistic. By that I meant that the energy is a sum total of the individual parts, plus the dividend that merged energy generates.

Then I drew a vertical rectangle and wrote the word MINISTRY within it. I added two arrows to note that this ministry is both to the congregational family and to the neighborhood, community, and world beyond. I explained that the rectangle represented the full scope of ministry of Centerville Church that would become possible by fully tapping the congregation's potential.

Then I drew a broad arrow left to right from the circle toward the rectangle, from the symbol of potential energy to the symbol of congregational ministry, to represent movement and flow of energy. This time I asked the group to picture the leadership and organizational life of the church as the vehicle or channel to allow potential to flow toward reality.

For Centerville Church, that final part of the drawing was the key, or perhaps more accurately, the starting point. I drew an arrow veering upward from the broader arrow and labeled it PROBLEM

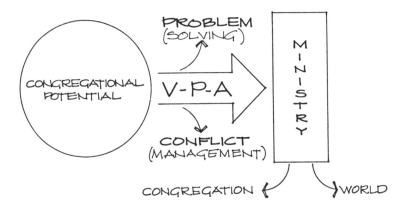

(solving), then a second arrow, veering downward, and labeled it CONFLICT (management). All organizations, because they are gatherings of people, have problems and create conflict. Effective leaders need problem-solving skills and conflict-management strategies, but problems constantly arise and multiply quickly. I then suggested an alternative to problem-solving and conflict-management ideas.

I used the four of us as an illustration. Suppose we felt a common calling to serve God in a particular project or ministry at the church. Suppose that each of us had a significant degree of clarity and energy and a strong sense of purpose and passion. Our common focus, when we met, would be on the vision, the developing plans, the work to do. We might discover along the way that we had differences of opinion on certain things, or that we had traits that were not particularly endearing. In fact, we might even have a history of disagreement or conflict among us. But as long as we maintained shared vision and commitment to a plan, and as long as each had tasks to carry out, we would move forward.

Now suppose, conversely, that the four of us had little or no vision or commitment, but that we often found ourselves together at the church. What would fill our time? Problems and conflicts would, in all likelihood, develop. People just standing around, with little motivation, inspiration, or sense of purpose, will as often as not generate problems and create conflict.

I ended up suggesting that if the leaders of Centerville Church worked on the bigger picture—mobilizing larger numbers of people from the congregation, tapping more fully congregational potential, envisioning clearer plans for ministry—many of their problems and conflicts would, if not disappear, at least stand in a different context.

## The Graphic as a Diagnostic Tool

These three elements—the circle, the rectangle, and the arrow—viewed in terms of the relative size of each, can be used as a diagnostic tool in assessing the overall life and ministry of a congregation. Two circles can be used to symbolize congregational potential. One circle is drawn with a solid line to represent the degree to which the church currently taps its potential, and the other drawn with a broken line representing what could be the full potential of the church. Two rectangles symbolize the scope of ministry of the congregation. One is drawn with a solid line to represent the present ministry of the church, and the other is drawn with a broken line representing the scope of ministry as it would be if the full congregational potential were tapped. Two broad arrows symbolize the organizational infrastructure of the church. One is drawn with a solid line to represent the present leadership and infrastructure, and the other is drawn with a broken line representing what would be a fuller, more appropriate infrastructure.

The specifics of this drawing may be adapted to each congregation's circumstances, as revealed in the three situations.

## Centerville Church

This congregation's story suggests the most frequent configuration of this graphic.

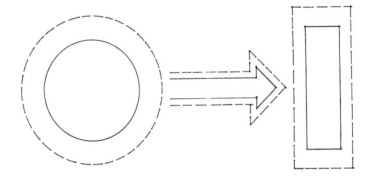

Centerville Church has experienced modest church growth in the last decade, new faces mingling with those of longer-term members on a given Sunday morning. Many programs listed in the Sunday worship bulletin or monthly newsletter were initiated some years ago, and participation has diminished. The organizational structure has remained largely intact for almost a generation. Newer members express a desire for a broader and more varied program offering as well as for some changes in the basic style and approach of the church. This congregation seems to be tapping substantially less than its full potential, to be developing a program life and ministry less than what is needed, and to have maintained an organizational structure unready to develop that fuller ministry of the future.

## St. Mark's Church

The graphic was quite different for St. Mark's Episcopal Church, where my friend and colleague David was serving as interim rector. Like many congregations located at the edge of a metropolitan area, this church had a proud history. Through much of its 135 years, it was a thriving parish, filling its large sanctuary on Sunday mornings, using Sunday school classrooms to their capacity, and offering program opportunities almost every night of the week, all in a beautifully maintained church plant and property. Decline had begun gradually in the 1960s and had become precipitous in the last fifteen years.

I was asked to lead a Sunday afternoon officers' retreat. Participants completed a pre-retreat questionnaire, listing their hopes and expectations for the gathering, which seemed broad and ambitious for such a small congregation, with a board of eight and a membership of about sixty-five. Some expressed hope and enthusiasm for a new and brighter future, though I sensed something forced and uncertain in the tone in which they wrote. Others were more forthright about their discouragement.

We gathered in the rectory and put on name tags, and I outlined my plan for the day. Then I gave them each a second name tag bearing an unfamiliar name, and a three-by-five card on which I had written an introduction to the "person" whose name they had been given. These were fictitious descriptions, but each one was representative of the residents in the neighborhood surrounding the church, most of whom had not been drawn to the church.

I asked the group to walk alone a block or two away from the church, wearing their second name tag, then to head back toward the church as if they were that person. I asked that they stop and note their impressions of the church as it first came into view. What does the church "say" from a distance? I asked them to pause again as they crossed the intersection at the edge of the church property, observing the overall setting—the trees, shrubbery, lawn, fencing, and signs—noting any impressions they had. What "message" did they get from the building and grounds?

I asked these officers to enter one of the gates that opened onto the church grounds, walking slowly enough to be mindful of their feelings as they took things in, and to be particularly mindful as

they walked up the steps at the main entrance, paused in the
vestibule, then entered the sanctuary.

We later gathered back in the rectory living room, and I asked
them to remain in their role and respond to some interview questions, which they did. This exercise gave them a fresh and clear,
affirming and troubling perspective on their church. I admired their
courage.

Then I introduced the graphic that had evolved from that breakfast meeting with the Centerville delegation. One of the St. Mark's
officers observed, "We are just too small a congregation trying to
sustain such a big and demanding a ministry." Others around the
circle nodded in agreement. After a remarkably candid conversation, an older woman who had served the church with devotion for
nearly half a century said with noteworthy clarity, "I think it is time
for us to rise to the challenge of leading this congregation in
grieving the ending of its life and work." Beginning with that
remarkable comment, the board began to offer that very leadership,
with artfulness and sensitivity, over the following months. The
Sunday after Easter, by their own choosing, David presided at their
last worship service as a congregation.

At one point in that afternoon's reflections, a member of the
board took a magic marker and adjusted my graphic, which was
still on the newsprint easel, to represent St. Mark's reality as he saw
it. He simply reversed the solid and dotted lines.

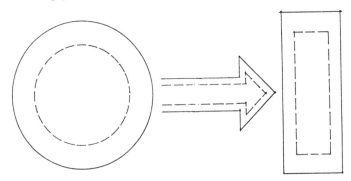

Although this might seem to be a narrative of discouragement
and defeat, I retell it often as a story of courage and faithfulness. A
few months after the vestry voluntarily handed their keys to the
bishop, the church was sold to an African-American congregation

that immediately thrived at that location. The sanctuary, church school rooms, and parish hall are alive again with life and vitality. The former members find that they return to warm and hearty hospitality, welcomed always as if they were dignitaries. Most have joined one of three nearby parishes, where they have been greeted with open arms. Though a certain sadness lingers, a sense of nobility prevails.

## Gladwyne Church

Congregations have life cycles, energy ebbing and flowing, flourishing times, then languishing times. Gladwyne Presbyterian Church experienced a burst of energy in the 1985–86 church year: new people, fresh ideas, and a rush of activity.

That momentum carried into the fall of 1986 but in the eyes of some took on a frenzied quality. "I like our 'airport, not airline' metaphor," complained one church member, "but sometimes it feels too much like an airport around here! It feels to me like we're running frantically, talking quickly, bumping into each other, getting more and more breathless." Enthusiasm had evolved, some observed, from contagious involvement into a troublesome epidemic of busyness. A certain rhythm, gracefulness, and balance were lost.

Sarah, who had come to the church seven years earlier, bringing gifts of creativity and energy, began a training program during that year to become a contemplative spiritual guide. Feeling a concern about this hyperactivity at the church, she began to pray. Quietly, like leaven, she invited others to join her in prayer. They started a sort of conspiracy to bring change to the congregation.

That fall the nominating committee asked Sarah to become an elder, a member of the board, and she accepted. Elders on the Gladwyne Board each had leadership and oversight responsibility for a program area, but Sarah was asked to be the "elder at prayer." She would take no leadership assignment, at least not for program. Her role evolved quickly. She arrived early for board meetings, set a simple altar with a candle, a cross, a Bible, and the elements of the Eucharist. In a quiet, undistracting, almost invisible way, she would pray as the board did its work. She called her role a "leadership of prayerful presence." She spoke only occasionally with suggestions like, "Maybe we ought to interrupt the discussion and take five minutes for quiet refection and prayer," which was usually timely and helpful.

At one meeting Sarah offered the proposal that the board name three weeks, spaced through the church year, to be designated as "sabbath weeks" during which the only activity on the church calendar would be worship and Sunday school for children. Her plan was implemented and became the cornerstone decision toward returning balance and gracefulness to the church's life and ministry.

The graphic as it applied to Gladwyne Church in this season of flurry and frenzy is identical to that of St. Mark's Church, but the story behind the graphic was very different. In St. Mark's case the critical mass of people was simply too small to maintain even a minimal worship and program life. In Gladwyne's case there was a vital group of people, but they had undertaken too ambitious and demanding a commitment.

I have added two elements to this graphic after its earlier presentations. Motivated people and inspired congregations—who name, tap, and focus their energy creatively and productively—seem to be carried by two currents.

The one I call "sending energy," which generates momentum—from *within*. People experiencing this kind of energy say things like, "Something just woke up inside me," or "I suddenly got turned on," or "I don't know where it came from, but I got fired up." Brian, a high school teacher and professional musician and singer, worked with at-risk high school students in Chester, Pennsylvania, in a

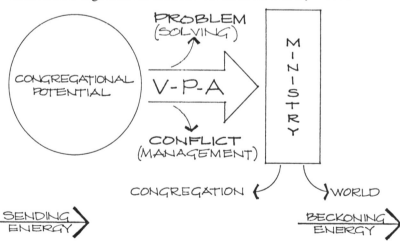

program called Learn and Earn, a part of Gladwyne Church's overall partnership with that highly depressed small city. "It's hard to explain," he said one day as we drove to Chester together, "but I heard about what people were doing in Chester, and one day 'the voice' said 'go,' and I did."

The other energy source for activating potential I call "beckoning energy," which invites—from *beyond* oneself. A woman in her mid-forties described her experience: "I was casually reading an article in the morning paper about conditions in Chester and the work of a newly formed community organization, and something called out to me. I folded the paper, got in my car, drove down there, and I've been volunteering two days a week ever since." A twenty-five-year-old graduate student said, "I don't know why, but the stories of battered or abandoned teenage girls have always brought tears to my eyes and an ache to my heart. When I saw their pictures, their eyes seemed always to be looking at me. I had to do something, so I began to work at a shelter in a nearby neighborhood." And a member of a small Baptist church reported, "It was as if our whole congregation, all of a sudden, stood up together to respond to the needs of families burned out by a fire in our community."

The Bible offers abundant examples of sending energy and beckoning energy, or some combination of the two. Paul told Timothy to stir the gifts of power and light within himself (2 Timothy 1:6-7). The apostle said that "suffering produces endurance, and endurance produces character, and character produces hope, and hope does not disappoint us" (Romans 5:3-5). Ananias reported, as he touched Paul's eyes and his sight returned, that he was sent to him by God (Acts 9:10-19). Isaiah, hearing the voice of God in the temple, said, "Send me" (6:1-8). Paul urged his readers to know themselves as "ambassadors for Christ" (2 Corinthians 5:20). Jesus "set his face to go toward Jerusalem" (Luke 9:51). The disciples responded to Jesus' invitation to "follow me," a man revealed in a vision beckoned to Paul from Macedonia, and Wise Men followed a star in the western sky.

Churches, as individual members and corporately as congregations, tap *sending* energy as they seek to discern call, giftedness, purpose, and passion. "When I know my heart, my heart knows the way," offered a church officer at a weekend leadership retreat. "It is as if my heart has a homing device within it," reflected a church member who had found her unique calling for ministry. Churches tap *beckoning* energy as they focus on mission, vision, goals, and objectives for faithfulness and ministry. "Once we wrote our vision statement, we could feel some profound source of energy release from deep within our congregation," a young pastor enthusiastically reported. "By naming our goals we seemed to take the first steps toward achieving them," added a church council member.

## Reaching Full Potential

Some church leaders tell exciting stories of congregational re-awakening, of congregational potential richly and deeply tapped. Others talk about congregations that are troublingly unresponsive even to promising strategies. I ask those who have witnessed revitalization and renewal to name ingredients that have contributed to the change. And I ask similar questions of the others: What is not happening? What qualities or dynamics seem absent? These leaders concur that twelve qualities or practices seem to stand out as being essential to successfully realizing the full potential of an individual or group.

- *Appreciation:* An atmosphere of hospitality, respect, and encouragement is fostered. People are called by name. Even when a task agenda is full, there is time for pastoral concern. Effort is recognized, and gratitude is frequently expressed.
- *Acceptance:* People, with their own unique style and experience, are welcomed. Differences are embraced. Team building is valued, and belongingness is nurtured.
- *Openness:* Everyone has opportunity to contribute, participate in decision making, and impact the process and the outcome. Democracy, or even consensus seeking, prevails. Power is fairly distributed and exercised.
- *Accomplishment:* Achievement is encouraged, supported, and celebrated, yet faithfulness is valued over success. Failures are accepted and learned from. People are challenged to strive for their personal best. Training and resources are readily available.
- *Positive spirit:* A climate of excitement and expectancy prevails. Laughter comes easily. The group is an enjoyable and safe place to be.
- *Spiritual groundedness:* A sense of something deeper

predominates. Faithfulness and spiritual discipline and discernment are valued. A commitment to prayerfulness and gracefulness is obvious.

- *Idea friendliness:* Creativity and innovation are welcomed and encouraged. A "let's give it a try" attitude prevails. Ideas are appreciated, built on, and linked. Tradition is preserved even as new ideas are explored.
- *Future orientation:* A sense of vision, calling, and mission, both as a basic orientation and in written statements, is clear. Goals are defined and plans are reasonable. A sense of anticipation and momentum is evident.
- *Clear leadership:* Leaders are inspired and inspiring, energizing, encouraging, and empowering. They embody as well as lead, are assertive but not controlling, and are trustworthy and competent. They understand and appropriately play their role.
- *Appropriate structure:* Organizational clarity, open communication, both formal and informal structures, crisp and effective meetings, and clear and helpful policies and procedures have been established.
- *Meaning seeking:* Motivation comes from a sense of urgency and significance, a belief that the work is purposeful, that the vision, goals, and plans contribute to some higher end.
- *Flexibility:* Policies and procedures serve people and program. Consistency is balanced with adaptability, a sense of definition yet a spirit of emergence.

*Chapter Ten*

# Governance from the Sacred Center
## Congregational Structure and Leadership

From the very beginning of my interim ministry work at Honey Brook Presbyterian, I encouraged members to bring their personal and collective vision into focus, to name their goals for ministry in the future, and to develop plans accordingly.

A longtime and respected leader of the church at a meeting of the board asserted that the board did not want to make any decisions until the new minister came, and others agreed with his position. But I offered an alternative: that the board make *all* the important decisions before the new minister came. At first hearing my idea made little sense to them, but they asked me to say more.

I explained a hunch I had about the last twenty years of ministry in this church, knowing that those present had served as leaders in the church across those decades and more. I proposed that years before, a new minister had come. He said, "Let's go that way," and the leaders said, "Okay, let's go," and off the congregation sailed in that direction. Some years later the next minister arrived. "No, let's go this way," he said, and folks reset their sails and off they went. Still later a third minister arrived. "How about that direction?" he urged, and they reset their sails still again.

I suggested that members must have felt somewhat waffled and buffeted, and that they followed at times with less than total enthusiasm. In fact, I guessed there were resisters among them and that it was not all that smooth a sail in any of those directions. As I finished my description, there were hearty nods of agreement.

Then I proposed that the board determine the basic calling of this church and lead the congregation in a prayerful process of clarifying its vision for the next ten years. Through a process of prayerful discernment, the church could set its goals, make its plans, get itself organized, and step forward toward that future. Then they could look for a minister who wanted to lead the congregation in the direction they wanted to take, where they believed God was leading them.

This was clearly new thinking to them, yet over the next two years, they constantly referred to that conversation. As the idea became clearer, it also became more appealing. And finally, the search committee completed its work, and the new minister was called. The church had done its work of visioning, goal setting, planning, and organizing, so when she arrived, they had a clearer sense, as a congregation, of their calling, their gifts, and their understanding of what it means to be led by the Spirit. They chose a leader ready to sail with them on a course they had set.

Now compare this story with another one. At age fifty-two, Dan was called to a large church in central Pennsylvania. This church had stayed downtown, maintained steady growth, increased racial and ethnic diversity, and developed a vital ministry in response to the needs of its neighborhood. This historic congregation had been known as a "big pulpit" church, and several former ministers had moved on to national reputation as preachers. The members viewed their past ministers as strong leaders, each in his own way. The church had, however, gone through some conflict during the most recent pastor's tenure. When Dan arrived, it was in significant disarray and seemed uncertain about where and how to move forward.

In the interview process the search committee made it clear to Dan that they wanted a decisive leader. Dan saw himself as just that. His leadership style was firm, his vision for the church clear, and his personal faith strong. He was clearly, it seemed, the right man for the job.

Two years after he began his work at this church, things were not going well for Dan. He struggled to sort out what had happened: "They said they wanted bold, evangelical sermons. They said they wanted me to lead decisively. They said they were ready to step forward under that kind of leadership. I guess they were wrong." He told me about his ministry in Virginia, then North Carolina. There, he had looked forward to preaching. The response to his ministry had been vigorous. Leadership was fun. Incredible things happened at each church. He expected his work here to be more of the same, maybe even better. He had been thrilled to be called to this church. What went wrong?

These stories belong together. Though the ministries had different outcomes, they unmask similar dynamics. I have sat in too many restaurants and listened to too many pastors and lay leaders say things tragically similar to Dan's lament. I have seen too many congregations play out, again and again, that early Honey Brook scenario. The situations and people have changed. But Harvey keeps swimming in his predictable circle.

The alternative is to dare to believe that the church—fully human, scarred and flawed—can be the people of God, ambassadors for Christ and agents of reconciliation. Our churches can be guardians of holy ground, truly the body of Christ. We who are called to faithfulness and leadership can know ourselves as inspired by divine will.

Envision your congregation as a total environment, an ecosystem. An ecosystem is a subtle blend of the stable and the evolving, the fixed and the fluid. It maintains its stability, yet, moved by longings and fresh possibilities that stir from within and buffeted by shifts and changes that impact from the outside, it changes. Sometimes it evolves, like a tadpole to a frog; sometimes it transforms, like a caterpillar to a butterfly. Picture your church as a huge mobile, all parts dancing together in harmony and balance. If a single piece were an ounce heavier or lighter, suspended a millimeter this way or that, the mobile would fall out of balance, until all the pieces readjusted to the system's new balance. Image your faith community as a molecule, many elements orbiting and vibrating around a nucleus, held in place by a delicate balance of attractions. "In Christ all things hold together," Paul wrote to the Colossians (1:17).

I outline in this chapter a "model-less model" of congregational leadership and organization. It is "model-less" in that it is, more than anything else, an approach or a perspective, rather than a program or a plan. It blends the structured and the spontaneous, the clear and the ambiguous, the fixed and the unfolding. It is a "model" in that it does offer a framework within which to do this work.

## The Center

As the title of this book suggests, organizational faithfulness begins at the sacred center and evolves outward. At this sacred center is Christ, wellspring of the Spirit, the heart of God, the divine. In this sense every church is Pentecostal—each founded on a date and at a location chronicled in its church history but birthed on the fiftieth day of Eastertide. Attentiveness to the sacred center must be larger than mere slogans about Christ-centeredness. It must entail real and generative experience and commitment of the people, as described in part 1.

Grounded and emerging from this divine center is the essence of the organizational life of the congregation: (1) core people, (2) core team, (3) core values and principles, (4) core charism, and (5) core vision. From these radiate the life and ministry of the church.

## Core People

At the heart of any faithful and effective congregation are core people. Perhaps this formula, adapted from Stephen Covey, captures their essence: C + C —> T(w).[1] That is: *character* plus *competence* leads to *trust(worthiness)*. Effective people, leaders, and organizations are rooted in a spirit of mutual trust and trustworthiness. Those who trust and are trustworthy combine two elements: character and competence. Character is broad, rich, and many faceted, deeper than personality or image, substantive and not simply cosmetic. Character has to do with integrity, authenticity, depth, and believability. A person of character is marked by genuineness, reliability, consistency, and congruence. True character can only be formed over time and is deepened by commitment and hard work.

Competence is a spectrum of skills already mastered and a commitment to continual learning. Commitment to competence is a value, something held in high regard. This is a matter of personal discipline and ongoing commitment. When members and leaders are committed to deepening character and broadening competence, trust grows, and trust is the bedrock of personal and organizational effectiveness.

## Core Team

Core people together form a core team—those who most fully hold in trust the community and its life. These are the stewards of the dream and guardians of the calling, those who resonate with the movement of the Spirit in and through the life of the congregation. They are committed to faithful discernment as well as careful decision making. They are motivated by personal clarity about their call, gift, purpose, and passion in service.

These people may or may not be church officers. They may serve the church in a variety of ways. Those who are part of this core team must not become an elite group, lest they manipulate or undermine the life of the church. They must be like leaven in the loaf. They are, in the best sense of the word, servant-leaders. Their loyalty to God, the church, and the people must be focused and steady. These people must be genuinely humble, discerning, and sensitive. In a certain sense these people are neither named nor elected. They simply are. To the degree that they become involved and influential in the leadership and organizational life of the church, the church may become that much more fully aligned with God's calling, more fully empowered and animated by God's Spirit. Identifying such people can be a sensitive matter, so it is important to approach that task with wisdom.

## Core Values and Principles

Core people know their church as if it were a person. They hold in trust the core values and principles of the congregation. These values and principles become life-giving when they are visible and clearly named. They must be embodied in behavior as well as stated in words. Renewed and renewing churches find that naming and embracing basic values and principles brings focus and coherence to the life of the congregation as well as clarity and energy to the ministry of the church.

## Core Charism

At the sacred center lies a discernment of the charism of this particular congregation. "Charism," a term less familiar to Protestants, is used more frequently by some Roman Catholic orders. The charism of an order—the Benedictines, Augustinians, or Jesuits, for example—combines the founding vision, the essential genius, and the integrative and cohering energy of that order. All churches share a common and foundational Christian calling—to preach the gospel, celebrate the sacraments, teach children and adults, offer pastoral ministry, reach out in love and service—a mandate of all churches of Jesus Christ. But individual churches also seem to have their own unique and particular call, giftedness, purpose, and passion—a charism.

## Core Vision

Finally, at the heart and soul of a congregation lies a core vision that, paradoxically, is both chosen and discovered, a matter of both decision and discernment. Chapter 11 will offer suggestions about how to discern and name that vision. Visioning must be an open-ended, ongoing, continuous, and generative process, though it may take the form of a specific vision statement in a given moment in time.

# From the Center Outward

In this "model-less model" there emanates from the sacred center a threefold ministry of leadership—inspiration, consultation, and celebration. In recent years, congregational leaders, especially clergy, have learned the language of empowerment. They know the slogans and speak them with apparent commitment, energy, and enthusiasm. In reality, however, little empowerment is being practiced. This approach might help your congregation turn words into action.

## Inspiration

Iain was a sporadic worshiper at the church and could not remember just why he attended church one particular Sunday. Sometimes he came to watch his son in children's choir, but they were not singing that day. His daughter was an occasional lay

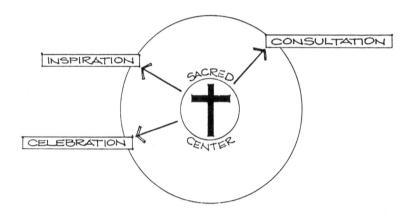

reader, but this was not one of her Sundays. Yet for some reason, which he later named as God's grace, he came that Sunday.

The guest preacher for the day was Father Roger Desir, an Anglican priest from Port au Prince, and a native Haitian. Members of a mission delegation from the church had met Roger some years before, and the congregation had recently raised $35,000 to establish a center in Haiti to support his work and the work of Christian base communities. Small teams from the church traveled regularly to Haiti to continue the work and deepen the partnership. Roger spoke with a quiet passion and a disarming faithfulness. The pain, courage, and devotion of the Haitian people were evident in Roger's words and demeanor.

At the end of the service, Iain, a man of typical Scottish reserve, threw his arms around me as tears ran down his cheeks. "Will you go with me to Haiti?" he wept. Three weeks later we flew together to that impoverished island country to initiate a partnership between pediatricians from the children's hospital in Philadelphia where Iain was chief of staff and their counterparts in Haiti.

One night halfway through our six-day stay in Port au Prince, Iain and I sat alone on the upstairs porch of our guest house, sipping after-dinner coffee and chatting. Lightning stabbed the night sky as cascading rains broke the grip of the intense heat of the day. "I don't often get to church, Howard," Iain began, "and I bet you think I don't hear much when I do. That's not true! There's a spirit at our church. It's hard to name. I'm not sure I can find words for it. But I can feel it," he continued. "That spirit has most touched me when people talk about their work in Haiti. But it broke through to me the Sunday that Roger spoke. I couldn't just watch anymore. I had to get involved."

It is hard to describe, but leaders create and communicate a climate of inspiration that begins with themselves. Inspiring people are themselves inspired. They draw people out and encourage them to come forward. They evoke the cornerstone elements of empowerment—passion and responsibility taking.

Inspired and inspiring leaders understand the nature and process of motivation—the human needs for achievement, affiliation, and influence. The fruit of inspiration includes a community of people who are active, assertive, animated, and involved. People in an inspiring atmosphere know that their responsiveness will be honored, affirmed, and empowered.

I frequently ask groups to define "leader" and "leadership." I have filled pages of newsprint with responses. The lists typically mix qualities and activities—but almost every group is surprised to note that two-thirds to three-quarters of the things they name are qualities, characteristics, and personal traits. And they are quick to link those traits to an ability to nurture an atmosphere in the church and with people. And as often as not the ingredient of atmosphere most vigorously named is inspiration. Leaders are responsibility takers, and they encourage others to follow, but the cornerstone quality out of which leadership activity seems to emerge is the capacity to inspire.

## Consultation

Evidently the adult education committee caught the spirit of the mission and outreach committee, and a "super market or farmer's market" story, not unlike the "airline or airport" story, became an animating metaphor for the group. Someone commented in a committee meeting one evening that the committee had been planning adult education programs as if we the church were a supermarket, trying to do all the buying, stock all the shelves, writing all the advertising, and set all the prices—and then entice the community to come in and shop. Others on the committee, also disappointed

with less than enthusiastic participation in the programs they offered, nodded in agreement.

Then a proposal was offered: What if we became a farmer's
market? The image seemed apt: At a farmer's market an owner
erects a large tent, constructs rows of different size stalls, paves a
parking lot, does some basic advertising, and then invites merchants
to rent space and sell their wares. The owner might help plan for an
appropriate variety of product lines and help create an attractive
place to shop, but otherwise the merchants are on their own.

From that meeting developed what one committee member, who
had an affection for long but engaging titles, called "the en-
trepreneurial approach to church program development." The process was simpler than the name. The committee changed its mandate.
It began by making public its assumption that people in the church
did want programs but quickly added that the committee could do
no better than merely guess what they might be. Then the committee
invited anyone with program ideas to come forward. The committee
did not, however, offer to plan or provide the programs that were
suggested but rather to help people who had ideas to carry them
forward. Within two years the program calendar was full of exciting
and well-attended events, and few were planned by the committee.
The committee continued to provide core courses in adult education, but electives were chosen, organized, planned, then offered by
ad hoc laity teams, which were encouraged, supported, and assisted
by the committee.

A pattern all too familiar to those who take leadership in program
development in local churches was suddenly broken. You probably
recognize the cycle: Someone comes to the pastor or adult education committee, saying, "We ought to have a program for young
adults . . . single mothers . . . separated and divorced people . . .
whatever." The pastor or a committee rushes to pull together a
program, announces it in the church newsletter, sets up twenty-five
chairs, puts on the coffee, and then only seven people show up. And
those who made the request are among the missing. And this is not
the first time it has happened. Frustration and resentment build. Yet,
methodically, congregational leaders play the script over and over
again!

Church leaders can inspire creativity and responsiveness, helping people from the congregation to "do their thing," rather than

doing things for them. To borrow some phrases from secular leadership literature, they encouraged "self-directed people" to become part of "self-managed teams."[2]

Inspiration coaxes individuals and then teams of people, who have linked passion and responsibility taking. These inspired people bring vision into focus, feel called and gifted, and have specific ideas to bring into being. Inspired people do not want someone to do it for them; they do not want to hand off their idea to someone else. They do want and need some assistance in order to do it themselves.

This work of support and assistance I am calling consultation has four ingredients:

1. *Set guidelines* that provide a way to get oriented and positioned and that clarify the rights and obligations of ministry teams. Self-managed teams may be granted substantial freedom, but that freedom might be required to be congruent with the vision, overall goals, and basic values and principles of the church.

2. *Encourage team building,* and provide assistance in learning how to value and implement collaboration, and how to develop and define roles and procedures for working together.

3. *Provide access to resources,* because effective self-managed teams need space and budget, equipment and supplies, knowledge and skills, personal coaching and support.

4. *Affirm accountability,* an obligation to all self-managed ministry teams to name publicly the vision, goals, and plans for their work. Teams should remain connected to the infrastructure of the church as they carry out their work, keep careful financial records, and share the results of their work at its conclusion.

Some teams might work in close communication with the standing bureaucracy of the church; some might work in more informal ways, as part of the adhocracy of the church. But in all cases a key dynamic is creating an inspiring atmosphere that calls forth people and teams of people enthusiastic about doing ministry, and then providing resourceful consultation.

## Celebration

Leaders of empowered congregations are liturgists of celebration. People want, need, and have a right to recognition, affirmation, and celebration.

In too many churches too many people work without relief as they "keep on keeping on." Inspired, encouraged, empowered self-managed ministry teams need times of celebration. Celebrating commitment and hard work, passion and responsibility taking—whether successful or not—is important.

Even ministries that are partial successes, or perhaps failures, require that people invest time and energy, demonstrate faithfulness, and struggle with feelings of disappointment. Churches can celebrate these efforts with those who felt called and dedicated to that work. Success is not the measure of faithfulness.

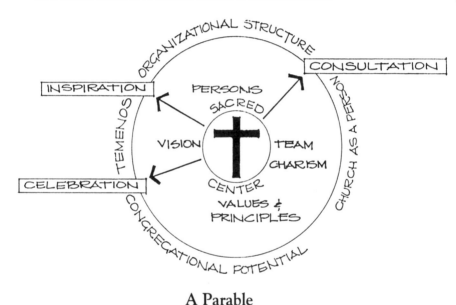

## A Parable

Finally, a parable from my experience characterizes a subtle but important dimension of this kind of leadership. When I go on personal retreat at a monastery in Canada, I often stay in a hermitage at the eastern point of a cove. I love to paddle a canoe onto the lake at dawn and watch the rising sun.

One day shortly after sunrise, the winds began to gust across the lake. As I paddled out of the cove toward the center of the lake, I was swept first this way and then that by the fresh wind. No matter how hard I paddled, I could not maintain my course. Shortly I found myself blown into a cluster of reeds along the south shore. As I pondered my dilemma, my eyes fell on a rock just below the surface of the water. I slid carefully out of the canoe, hoisted the rock from the lake bed, and lowered it gently into the bow of the canoe. I slipped back onto the wicker seat and made my way back out onto the lake.

The rock settled the bow of the canoe deeper into the water. I resumed paddling at full strength, turning my paddle slightly at the end of each sweep to hold the course. It was then that the experience became a parable, another metaphor. I had spent much of my leadership life paddling hard. I would fight hard, turning this way and that, frantically paddling on the left side, then the right, then back to the left again, getting more and more exhausted. Leadership became breathless and tiring for me and others. What would happen, I wondered, if I became like the rock in that canoe? What if I became ballast, something that gives stability and steadiness? A new way of being a leader began to become clear.

I think of this new way as simply being present. It is nothing dramatic. Indeed, that is just the point. It is a matter of simply and quietly "being there." Since that day, I have paddled less. I navigate less. I overwork and overgive less. And paradoxically, my leadership seems to have become more effective and more empowering.

*Chapter Eleven*

# Vision, Plan, and Action
## Strategic Planning from the Sacred Center

In the previous chapter I presented the congregation—its membership, leadership, and organizational structure—as an ecosystem—holistic, stable yet evolving, and organic. I have viewed empowerment and partnership with high seriousness. Ultimately, however, the call to empowerment is beyond theory, beyond even vision and plan. It is a call to action. "He has showed you, O mortal, what is good, . . . but to do justice and to love kindness and to walk humbly with your God," Micah insisted (6:8). "Let justice roll down like waters, and righteousness like an everflowing stream," thundered Amos (5:24). "Each tree is known by its own fruit," Jesus taught (Luke 6:44). "When I was hungry, . . . thirsty, . . . a stranger, . . . naked, . . . sick, and in prison," Jesus reassured the surprised ones who were invited into the kingdom (Matthew 25:42-43). This is a call to faith and works, to incarnation, to making love concrete and visible. It is about "walking the talk."

## Workers and Leaders
When I pack for a leadership event, I generally throw in a half dozen pages of dog-eared newsprint sheets, the ones I am most apt to find timely no matter what the group. Here is one that makes its way to the front wall of most every event.

The inner circle represents the core leadership of your congregation: the pastoral staff; the officers of the boards; your steady,

reliable leaders, some elected and some not. The next circle represents that cadre of faithful and dependable "good workers" who can
be counted on to come forward as needs arise. The third circle
represents those in the church who may or may not worship
regularly or contribute financially but who rarely come forward to
serve. When I describe this third group at a workshop, people nod,
and their faces speak of frustration and annoyance. Finally, the
outermost circle represents the unchurched people of your community whom you would love to reach and welcome. Here again
people nod their agreement.

These reactions are quite typical. The two inner circles are almost
always perceived by workshop participants as smaller than they
wished. Because those gathered usually belong in one of these
circles, they are eager to plan ways to "get the others in." Comments
about those in the outer circles range from curiosity to frustration
to resentment. Those in the inner circles are just as quick to
acknowledge that past strategies, even those that seemed laden with
promise, have largely failed.

They are also anxious to hear ideas about how to solve their
problem. This is often a good time to tell the "Harvey story"—to
caution against not simply "swimming faster" in familiar and
predictable and fruitless circles. To further encourage a new way of
thinking, I may share the "airline or airport" story or other metaphors at this point. I ask them to step back, to look at the larger
picture, to ponder the possibility of a different perspective. The

following narrative, drawn from my work with one church, describes many churches.

The elders of Union Church had become resentful, quickly sarcastic, and discouraged with the noninvolvement of a substantial portion of their membership. They expected me, as their interim minister, to suggest some ways to change that. Drawing on newsprint, I created four vertical columns on a fresh sheet. From left to right I headed them: "leaders," "managers," "workers," and the "uninvolved." (Sometimes when I make this presentation, I change the first two categories to "leaders-of-leaders" and "leaders.")

| LEADERS | MANAGERS | WORKERS | THE UNINVOLVED |
|---------|----------|---------|----------------|
|         |          |         |                |
|         |          |         |                |

I explain the difference between leaders, managers, and workers, using illustrations from a variety of arenas. For example, a carpenter is a worker, a foreman is a manager, and the general contractor is the leader. A salesman, the regional sales supervisor, and the vice president of sales fill similar roles. Or, thinking about the church, a worker may volunteer to plant bulbs in the church garden, but the chairperson of volunteers manages a corps of workers, and the trustee or board member in charge of church property is the leader.

We then discuss the qualities or characteristics, roles and typical tasks, and appropriate responsibilities that fall under each category. Readers might take some time to work with each of these categories, as well. After you have listed a number of characteristics, roles, tasks, and responsibilities in each column, see whether they cluster in any natural way. See whether there are four to six that seem basic and essential.

Initially the board members of Union Church addressed the characteristics of workers. Workers should be dedicated, faithful, committed, dependable, hardworking, and reliable.

Then they began to address the other columns. With much hesitation, they suggested that a leader has vision and inspires others, is a good organizer, gets others to help out, gives direction, and is trusted.

My next question is more difficult: How do you see yourself—

| Leaders | Managers | Workers | The Uninvolved |
|---|---|---|---|
| 1. *Vision:* They have vision and promote visioning in and from others. They encourage congregation-wide visioning. | 1. *Teams:* They gather those of like calling and vision, those who desire to work together, into cohesive and effective teams. They are encouragers and resourcers. They support and celebrate. | Heeding call, gift, purpose, and passion; serving freely, joyfully, and lovingly; motivated by faithfulness more than duty, obligation, or guilt; working alone or with others; finding a rhythm of work and rest, they are dedicated, resourceful, thorough, dependable, hard working, and inspired and inspiring to others. | Perhaps feeling disenfranchised, not listened to, manipulated, the target of endless strategies to get them involved, these may be resourceful people who are ready, awaiting an invitation to discern their call, gift, purpose, and passion for serving. |
| 2. *Inspiration:* They are inspired and inspiring, creating an atmosphere of safety, a climate of openness and trust. They are motivators and encouragers. | 2. *Structure:* They know how to build and use both formal (bureaucracy) and informal (adhocracy) organization. | | |
| 3. *Presence:* They emote a sense of integrity, authority, trustworthiness, and faithfulness. | 3. *Process:* They have mastered and effectively use a set of process skills, including decision making, problem solving, goal setting, action planning, and conflict managing, using or teaching them in a various settings. | | |
| 4. *Perspective:* They see both the whole and the parts and keep in mind the whole system. | 4. *Collaborative:* They relate to, communicate with, and resonate with leaders, other managers, and the workers in the congregation. | | |
| 5. *Direction:* They give basic direction and set broad goals, naming areas of priority. | | | |
| 6. *Process:* They are process leaders, better at questions than answers, more empowering than merely powerful. | | | |
| 7. *Structure:* They work with others to develop formal and informal structures. | | | |

VISION ──────→ PLAN ──────→ ACTION

your basic abilities and where you are most comfortable? Are you a worker, a manager, or a leader?

The Union Church group was neither embarrassed nor hesitant. Six of the nine saw themselves as workers, two cautiously offered themselves as managers, and only one announced himself as a leader. Soon one of the board members observed, "I guess we can't complain that we don't have so many workers if we don't have many leaders."

Their answers to my next question, How did each of you come to be an elder anyway? would probably be heard in any church board. "I've always been a dedicated worker," one shared, "so they said I'd make a good elder." Another explained, "Someone called from the nominating committee and almost pleaded, 'We're having such a hard time filling the slots. Please, take a turn. It's only three years. Say yes, please.' I like the person who made the call, so I said yes." And yet another person was persuaded to serve by the argument, "It will only mean one more meeting a month." Friendly, dedicated church workers had been "promoted" or "ambushed" to leadership, with neither the desire nor skill to serve in that role.

I have asked hundreds of people—congregational and judicatory leaders, seminary students and workshop participants, and many others—to participate in this exercise. The summary on page 153 shows the collective wisdom of those leaders. The work is evolving, and perhaps you can supply something that is missing.

Develop an increasing number of visionary and inspiring leaders, dedicated and competent managers, and watch the participation of the previously uninvolved increase, sometimes dramatically. The majority of strategies designed to involve and energize either inactive members or the unchurched in the community serve only to promote and perpetuate what I call a "producer-consumer mentality" in the church. What can we do, what program can we offer, what change can we make, what new "product" can we "produce" to "get them in"? I am proposing an alternative—*to work from the inside out.* Recover your sacred center as a congregation; renew and deepen your core team; revisit your core values and principles; reaffirm your basic charism and vision. Then ground leadership in this recovering of the sacred center.

At this point in the workshop I superimpose lines across the four categories, angling out from a point to the left of the column marked *leaders,* forming a broadening angle. These lines suggest as they open to the right that there is a direct relationship between the number of leaders, then managers, then willing workers in the church—and the increased engagement of the uninvolved.

Recovering the sacred center creates possibility in a church. But it is not enough to remain in the center, as we observed earlier. We need to act, to do justice, to feed and clothe and comfort. The movement from potential to reality, from faith to works suggests a three-phase process—vision, planning, and action. The process must be comprehensive, focused, and workable. Yet I hasten to point out that as eagerly and confidently as we may dream and plan, life unfolds, as we all know, with a mind of its own. We can take initiative, clarify vision, set goals, make plans, and carry them out—but we should not be surprised by the unexpected.

## A Case in Point

George was a mover and shaker, a man of action who knew how to get things done, a successful businessman, a no-nonsense member of various not-for-profit boards, and one of the leaders of Gladwyne Church. He was a vigorous advocate of capitalism in contrast to my "loving criticism" of democratic capitalism. An unexpected result found its genesis in a conversation we had one day in which he stated bluntly that I thought all capitalists lacked compassion. My reaction was, "Then let's get some of the 'compassionate capitalists' together." The adhocracy clicked into gear. George gathered a group of eight businesspersons together the next week, and momentum started to build almost immediately. Their group became known officially as the Compassionate Capitalists, and they made a commitment to explore the form that compassion might take for them in terms of a specific project or ministry. In a couple of weeks George and his wife, Linda, met with me and related the progress the group was making. "We remembered Marvin Lewis, that fellow from the Ludlow section of Philadelphia who spoke at church one Sunday last year. We went to see him, and you won't believe it. He has a dream almost exactly the same as the one that's been brewing in us about housing in Ludlow."

The three of them set the process in motion. They met with the neighborhood's city councilman, local police, interested church and civic leaders, and even the mayor. Working together they brought a vision into focus—thirty-five houses in five years! Since then they have received two HUD grants, the most recent for $1.5 million. Six houses are completed and occupied, and ground has been broken for twenty more. Future projections calls for an additional twenty-five. A community once marred by division and in-fighting has forged visible and vigorous coalitions around a number of shared needs. It took from 1986 to 1994 for George, Linda, and the others involved to see the ribbon cutting for the first house, and the road was often steep. At times it even threatened to be a dead-end street, but they persevered. They were able to move outward from the sacred center of the church and put their faith to work.

## Vision

The "washer game" is simple and fascinating. Tie a length of thread about twelve inches long to a dime-sized washer. Hold the other end of the thread between your thumb and index finger about eye level, about twelve inches from your face. Keeping your fingers virtually still, moving them so imperceptibly that someone watching would hardly notice, make the washer swing back and forth, left to right. Then, just as subtly, let the washer come to rest. Now repeat the exercise, this time making the washer move in an arc away from you and back, then bringing it to rest again.

Now fix your eyes on the washer. The task of your fingers this time is to keep the washer absolutely still. But you are going to use your mind. Imagine that the washer is beginning to swing back and forth, left and right, the way you intentionally made it move the first time. Picture it beginning to move, remembering that the task of your fingers is to remain still. Watch, perhaps with surprise. Invariably, the washer begins to move, left and right, as if it had a mind of its own! Finally, picture the washer coming to rest. You will likely be just as surprised to see it come to rest as you were to see it start moving.

Movement is inclined in the direction we are looking, whether we look with our outer or our inner eyes. There is something to the idea of "self-fulfilling prophecy" in this.

Faithful and effective ministry is grounded in vision. Just as a person is different from his or her personality and hope is different from hopes, however, so vision is different from visions. A personality is a vehicle, a servant, an expression of a person; person is essence, and personality is existence. Hope is an attitude, an inner confidence, something invisible and unseen. Hope births hopes, possibilities, and aspirations. Vision is a mind-set, an outlook, an attitude. From vision spring visions.

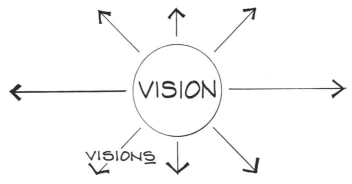

It is tempting for organizations and congregations in a planning mode to move too quickly to goals, objectives, specific plans, and strategies. This hasty narrowing and premature focusing eliminates a broader spectrum of possibilities and may sacrifice creativity and wider participation in the interest of time. The role of vision is broad, rich, and many faceted.

Vision bonds, connecting people and engendering community. It empowers, releasing and focusing energy. And it impassions, evoking deep caring and disciplined commitment. Vision communicates importance, inspiring urgency and immediacy. Vision is a rudder, giving direction. It focuses, setting and maintaining priorities; stirs aspiration, generating a spirit of possibility; and creates ownership, arousing loyalty and dedication. Vision is natural and exhilarating and trust building.

## A Personal Mission Statement

Leaders, called to be guardians and stewards of vision and visioning, must themselves be visionary. Congregational leaders, therefore, need to have a personal mission statement. They need periodically to discern their call to faithfulness, gifts for service, clarity of purpose, and passion for ministry. I have shared the following exercise with hundreds of congregational leaders in scores of churches. You need only a comfortable place to sit and a sheet of paper and a pencil.

Settle comfortably into your chair. Deepen your breathing, set aside distractions, and release any tension you feel in your body. Respond to these questions in an unrushed and reflective way. No judgment or criticism is implied. Insight is the goal. (In a workshop setting I ask these questions at a gentle pace, inviting people to write in playful ways, not worrying about spelling or sentence structure or staying on the lines, reminding them that no one will read what they write. I warn them that I will likely ask each question before they are finished with the one they are working on. I invite them to "let their hand write on its own," to let responses just kind of tumble out.)

Imagine gathered in front of you all the responsibilities you have undertaken at the church. Become aware of committees, task forces, or other work groups you serve on. Think of all those things to which you have been assigned or for which you have volunteered. Imagine the sum total of these commitments of time and energy. Now gently but firmly set them aside. Imagine picking them up and placing them on a table just to the right of your chair. You have not pushed them away or discarded them. Just set them aside for a moment. The space before you is now open and clear. You are free in this moment of any responsibility. Respond to these questions mindfully and unhurriedly.

1. What are you good at? Boast. Brag. Aim for no less than twenty characteristics or abilities in three minutes. Do not let your parents look over your shoulder and tell you not to brag. Go ahead. What are you good at? If in doubt, write it down.

2. Remember times of accomplishment in your life, of achievement or success. Big things or small things. I learned to recite the alphabet, ride a two-wheeler, water ski; I got an A in history, I got into college, I made the dean's list; I got promoted, I won an award, I made the quota; I proposed and she said yes; I lost ten pounds; I paid off the mortgage. In these times of accomplishment, what skills, abilities, traits, or personal qualities were called forth? I became more than I was before.

3. Remember times of adversity in your life, times of struggle and pain, burden and challenge—big or small. I repeated first grade. I flunked algebra. I was grounded for a month. My dog died, or my

aunt or grandpa or mom. I have a birth defect. I'm clumsy. I have a chronic illness. I lost my job. My marriage failed. My son is addicted to drugs. I've battled alcohol or depression or anxiety. But now think about what happened as a result of this adversity. You came through it. You're likely to be more than you were before the adversity. What characteristics, abilities, or gifts were forged in you in the midst of adversity?

4. You have just been handed an envelope containing a thousand dollars—ten crisp hundred dollar bills, with only this stipulation: You must give it away personally in the next twenty-four hours. You cannot write a check and send it by mail. You can deliver all thousand dollars to one location or pick ten separate recipients—individuals in need or organizations whose work you admire. Where would you deliver the money?

5. You have never been sure why, but there are certain kinds of human need that "get to you," that open your heart and send tears down your cheeks. When you hear of this kind of need in the news or see it in person or read about it in a book, you get a lump in your throat and an ache forms in your chest. Something in you responds and wants to reach out. Jot down some thoughts about these people and needs.

6. Suppose you had the gift of three extra hours a week that you could use to serve others. Where would you sign up? Suppose you had the gift of a day a week to offer in service. Where would you spend that day? Better yet, arrangements have been made so that you can have three months off from all responsibilities, and all expenses paid, to go anywhere on the planet to serve people in need. Where would you go?

7. You are at an awards dinner in your community just one year from today, and the "Mother Teresa Humanitarian Award for Loving Service" is about to be presented. The emcee opens the envelop and reads your name! Humbly but with a broad smile, you come forward. What have you done in the previous year to make you a worthy recipient?

8. You walk to your car and find what appears to be a sheet of notebook paper on the ground by the door. It's a page from God's notebook, and on it are written God's hopes and plans for your life in the next year. What is God trying to do in and through you in the months ahead?

9. To whatever extent these words make sense to you, ask yourself how you are being called by God, how you have been and are gifted, what your present sense of purpose in your life is, and where your passion (your energy, your natural enthusiasm) is. Let yourself catch the spirit as well as the content of your responses.

10. If you had a clean slate, no prior commitments or obligations, what do you really want to do to serve others? What would you just love to do?

11. Finally, let yourself begin to write a personal mission statement for the next twelve months. Look gently over everything you have written, reading the lines and between the lines as well. Dare to have a sense of destiny, of high calling, of divine mandate. Feel no obligation to finish this work now but let some clarity and momentum form.

Now set your pad and pencil and this work aside, placing all these thoughts on a table to your left, allowing the space in front of you to be free and open once again. With your left hand reach and hold the work you have placed on that table—your sense of call, gift, purpose, and passion, and your emerging personal mission statement. Let all of this settle into the palm of your left hand. Now, with your right hand reach and pick up those tasks and responsibilities you had placed on that table. Without rushing, letting the wisdom of your body join the reflections of your mind, bring your two hands into a pose that reflects how the two relate for you. Let yourself shift and move and experiment. You may settle on a single pose, like a statue. You may find a movement, a hand dance, that tells the story. Is there a message in this pose or movement?

I have asked several hundred people, mostly leaders in local churches, to do this exercise. In the majority of poses I have observed, hands are positioned far apart, often with fully outstretched arms. Though I am aware that this exercise may have been unsettling, I suggest that if we find our hands far apart, we will likely become quickly frustrated and burned out doing the work of our right hand—our obligations and commitments. And we will likely feel appropriately guilty for being unfaithful to the beckon of our left hand—our calling and giftedness, purpose and passion.

When I work with the leadership team from a congregation, I am likely to return to the newsprint, and write these letters:

$$\boxed{\text{A - A - R - V}} \quad OR \quad \boxed{\text{C - G - P - P}}$$

I ask group members to think about all of those commitments and responsibilities they held in their right hand, the things they do and the positions they hold. Then I ask, How did you first come to do that work or hold that office? The answers can often be found in one of four categories—they were Assigned, Appointed, or Recruited, or they Volunteered. "I was elected to our official board, then appointed to the property committee, the only slot that was open," is a frequent response. "I joined the church, and because I am a school teacher, I suppose, I was assigned to the Christian education committee." "I like Sarah, so when she asked me to help her out I just couldn't say no." "No one else offered, so I figured I could do it."

Then I make a challenge: Banish appointing, assigning, recruiting, and volunteering from your organizational glossary! "But where would I ever get Sunday school teachers if we did that?" a Christian education chairperson might respond. And then I offer another challenge: What are you saying about your teaching staff when you ask that question—about them and the quality of their teaching and their dedication as teachers?

It often seems timely to do some teaching about call—reflecting on the biblical word for church, *ecclesia* in Latin, *ekkaleo* in Greek, the "called out ones." We are called to faith and faithfulness, and each believer is specifically and individually called. We also need to reflect on gift—remembering that "gift" is from the root *charis* or "grace"—the gift of grace by which believers are called, then the gifts *(charismata)* that emerge from each believer as fruits of grace.

Thinking about call and gift in these ways can disrupt the current deployment of leaders. Leaders may well decide to a redirect their energy and priorities. Officers have been known to resign from roles and responsibilities that they now discern as unfaithful to their deeper calling, and to shift their leadership to new areas. Or some decide it is time for a sabbatical from any form of leadership at all!

These are crucial moments in individual and congregational decision making. Commitment to faithfulness and a deep desire to be attuned to God's leading must precede any organizational structuring, visioning, goal setting, or action planning. Only leaders who seek first a clarity of vision—attentiveness to personal Call, Gift, Purpose, and Passion—are ready to inspire vision and visions in the congregation. This work is an art. It means maintaining an ongoing, constantly nurtured spirit of visioning, and using specific strategies for making visioning concrete.

## Creating Vision Statements

The core leadership team of the church appropriately shepherds the process of writing a vision statement. It should do so in the context of temenos, a quality of space and community, as well as within a clearly defined and prayerfully formed infrastructure. Visioning begins with individuals who seek clarity about their own vision or purpose statement. It continues with visioning work as a leadership team. But this work must be fully open to the collective mind and heart of the entire congregation, and the total membership must be engaged in providing the data on which a more formal vision statement is based.

There are ways that visioning ought not be done. One congregation had an officers' retreat. They worked hard together on a visioning process, wrote an articulate and stirring vision statement, printed it in calligraphy on paper suitable for framing, and mailed it to the congregation. Then they wondered why it evoked so little allegiance. The board of another church virtually suspended new program development, asked church leaders to "wait until we finish the mission statement"—and wondered why resentments built and why the completed statement was quickly forgotten. The pastor of a third church convened a board meeting for the purpose of framing a mission statement, brought to the table with him a well-written draft that needed only minor revision—and the leaders wondered why the finished product inspired no one.

Leadership of the visioning process falls to the core team, but this work must be ongoing and it must engage a full cross section of the congregation. Effective leadership teams develop and implement a variety of specific strategies to do this visioning work throughout the congregation. Only when envisioning engages broad participation, when it evokes true concurrence and commitment, what someone has called "enlistment," is it truly generative and life-giving. It is a fascinating irony that the time span during which a vision statement is being written is often lively and energized, while the time following its completion is often lethargic and listless.

# Plan

My friend Bo is an artist. He paints on huge canvases, some as large as eight by fifteen feet. We got to talking one day about the creative process as we shared a bag lunch in his studio.

"In a certain sense painting is easy," Bo said. "I'm a visual person, so a potential canvas appears first in every detail in my mind's eye. I need only take brush and transfer the painting to the canvas. But it's not that simple," he went on. "Like that painting over there," he said, pointing to a recently completed piece. "To the right, where you see that old stone bridge, there was to be a little boy. He was very clear in my mind, five or six years old, in a yellow striped shirt, pushing his tricycle. But work as I would, he refused to enter the painting. And that man leaning on the split rail fence, he sort of arrived from behind the canvas, so I painted him in." Bo continued, "I've signed that painting. It's finished. My agent will sell it, and I'll gladly cash the check. But in a very real way it's not mine. I put brush to pigment and canvas, but brush, pigment, and canvas each has its part in the finished work. And so does . . . what shall I call it? The muse? The spirit? The Great Painter?" His voice trailed off.

Paradox is clearly at work in this process called planning. In a more "command and control" era of management, plans would be dictated, then monitored until they become reality. Management by Objectives, at its peak of popularity a decade or two ago, made it all appear so simple: name the objective, plot the pathways between here and there, then plan the journey. This seemed, and may still seem, persuasive and logical. The problem is it does not work! We cannot dissolve the planning department or abdicate the planning task. Planning is important, but there is a certain mystery to it.

## Three Metaphors

Earlier we referred to the "sowing/reaping paradox." Sow here—turning the soil, planting the seeds, watering and tending, only to reap over there—harvesting richly, but not, it seems, where we sowed. Yet I am convinced that the sowing and reaping are connected. An elder at a leadership retreat observed, "Planning is important. If you don't plan, little will happen. But don't expect exactly what you planned to happen." His comment captures the paradox well. Keep sowing, keep naming goals and objectives, keep planning, work hard to carry plans out, be intentional and focused. At the same time be watchful for surprises. Good things may happen that at first glance have no apparent connection to the work you have been doing. But in some mysterious and paradoxical way, there is a connection.

Others call it the "ready, fire, aim paradox." Contrary to the common expression, "ready, aim, fire," rocket science and NASA may be right: ready, fire, aim. The first and most urgent task in space exploration is to break out of the earth's gravitational pull. A rocket is fired, all energy devoted to optimum thrust, aimed in the general direction of the orbit. The course-correction phase comes next, then continues throughout the flight.

A pastor I met at a planning seminar offers a third metaphor, one that became meaningful to her on a visit to England, where she had the opportunity to try to find her way out of a hedgerow maze. She was led, blindfolded, to the center of the maze, where she was joined by four others. "We seemed immediately stymied," she recalls. "There were four directions to choose from, and we didn't know where to start. Then one of my companions spoke up," she continued. "'I suppose there's no way to know which one will lead us out,' the woman said, 'so I guess we ought to just pick one and start walking.' Out of that comment came our motto: Keep walking." That is not a bad motto for planning. Choose directions as best you can, but in any case, *keep walking*.

Visioning, goal setting, and planning set a direction, create momentum, and get the process started, but frequent midcourse correction will be needed. Christian base communities call this the "circle of praxis," a rhythm and cycle—first planning and action taking, then reflecting and pondering, then refocusing and redirecting, and finally, taking action once again. Two generations ago Reinhold Niebuhr reminded us that the church sets penultimate goals, while only God knows the ultimate goals.[1] Sometimes I think that we are called to give God the gift of momentum—visioning, goal setting, planning, and action taking the best we can, and praying that God (re)directs our plans and actions en route, knowing that it is easier to steer a moving object than to get a standing one started. And in reality, it may be only after the fact that we can discern what the goals and plans really were anyway.

Although the core team leads the visioning process—naming broad goals, general direction, or areas of emphasis for the future—these leaders must resist the temptation to micromanage. Planning is most appropriately and effectively done at the self-managed team or committee level. Too many leaders, pastors and church boards, try to vision and plan. They want to set the agenda, define the goals, announce the plans, then recruit laity to carry them out. Put simply, that is not working! People want access to the workshop and the tools, but they want to bring their own designs.

In churches committed to empowerment, partnership, and transformation, it is important to help people choose their time and place and way of serving. The fourfold discernment process—focusing on call, giftedness, purpose, and passion—can give basic definition to the Christian life as members of a community seek to live it. Few congregations, however, appear ready to take that kind of discernment process seriously.

An upstate New York church provides an illustration. As is the case with many congregations, the leaders at this church work hard to get people involved in the life and ministry of their church. They fall, however, into the "recruit volunteers trap." Leaders need followers, and planners need workers, so they typically approach people about volunteering. Unfortunately, they are successful! Responsibility taking begins to disconnect from passion. Some of these volunteers prove to be steady and committed workers, so they get promoted to become chairs of committees, leaders of task forces, conveners, and organizers. No one notices or honors their reluctance. "I suppose someone has to do it," the recruiter and the recruited find themselves saying. Passion and responsibility taking veer more widely apart. Driven by loyalty and doggedness, these faithful workers persist. The nominating committee, always alert for potential new leaders, spots them. These tireless yet tired workers feel honored by the invitation to serve on the official board. Though uncertain about their role and mandate, and increasingly out of touch with their calling, gifts, purpose, and passion, they say yes. Passion and responsibility taking are now totally severed from one another. This is an all too familiar sequence of things in all too many churches.

Self-managed teams (task forces, committees, mission groups)—guided by the vision statement and then the general direction, areas of emphasis, and broad goals named by the core leadership team—need to be supported, encouraged, and provided with resources. The church board does not *do* strategic planning; it *teaches* strategic planning.

The following model offers a basic template from which leaders and planners can learn goal-setting, decision-making, problem-solving, and action-planning skills.

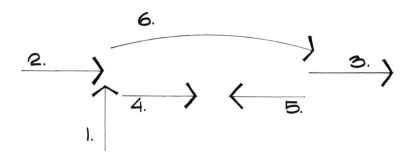

## 1. Where are we now?

Congregations need invitation and assistance to clearly and courageously name their present reality. This means removing lenses of optimism or pessimism to form an objective profile. It means diligently reviewing the life and ministry of the church. Who are we? What do we do, and why? Who are we as a corporate personality?

Then, more particularly, where are we as a committee, task force, or work team? What do we know to be our mission and mandate? How have we been functioning as a team, and how have we been fulfilling our mission? Each ministry team is invited and challenged to do regular and vigorous self-assessment.

Reflecting on where we are is the first step in writing or rewriting a mission statement. We need to define what we do and why we do it—now.

## 2. How did we get here?

What is our story? In chapter 7 I suggested strategies to explore heritage and history by telling the congregation's stories, and discussed the gifts such sharing can bring to the church. Like a person, the church has been molded and shaped by its past. The church has habits and characteristics, and patterns of thinking, feeling, and behaving formed long ago and continually reenacted. Exploring congregational history can be illuminating, liberating, healing, and empowering.

In the same way, each individual team at work within the congregation, whether formal or informal, must be aware of its history, so that the past may become a source of momentum into the future.

## 3. Where do we want to be?

What is our vision for the future? What is our sense of destiny and divine mandate? What calling, directing, and working do we discern God to be doing in and through us?

Individual work teams, inspired and guided by the vision statement and broad goals, must name their own vision, then work to clarify specific goals and objectives. They must imagine a future in which all that they have envisioned, the goals and objectives they have named, are realized. (Remember the washer game: Movement is inclined in the direction we envision!) They should be able to articulate in a conversation with a potential new member of the team what the team is working to accomplish. A vision statement, simply defined, states what we will be doing and why we will be doing it—in the future.

## 4. What moves us in that direction?

What are the driving forces? During World War II, social scientist Kurt Lewin developed what he called force field analysis. A simple image may make the point. Imagine holding a pencil vertically between four extended fingers of your left hand and four extended fingers of your right hand. If the pencil is suspended without movement, then the pressure exerted by each set of fingers is the same. To move the pencil, say, left to right, either the pressure from the left hand's fingers must be more forceful, or the fingers of the right hand must become less resistant. Either strategy will allow the pencil to move.

Apply this simple physics principle to the desired movement of a committee, task force, or congregation. Name the influences, forces, circumstances, or people already in place that support movement toward the desired goal. Might you add new driving forces or increase the forward press of existing forces?

## 5. What is pushing against us?

What are the restraining forces? What influences, forces, circumstances, or people are resisting or blocking forward movement? Can those forces be eliminated or diminished? Experience seems to suggest that working to reduce restraining forces is often a more fruitful strategy than trying to increase driving forces. Instinctively, pushing seems to evoke pushing back. Working to reduce resistance seems more inviting, less combative, thus more effective.

## 6. What's the plan?

Dissatisfied with where we are, inspired by our vision of where we might go, propelled by the trajectory of our past, conscious of what both encourages and resists movement, we develop an action plan. This planning process itself will have several stages, each with its own tasks: convening and building a team, deploying people and resources, developing time lines, conducting meetings, monitoring progress, and making midcourse corrections.

Planning inevitably involves change. And people have decidedly mixed feelings about change. I find it helpful to bring to the surface and name these feelings about change. My colleague and friend Gil Rendle points out that change is the antidote to what is lifeless and boring about stability, and stability is the antidote to what is disruptive and threatening about change. Living and growing people and congregations creatively balance the two![2]

One of the questions I frequently ask people is, What are the ingredients necessary for creative change to take place? The responses I have heard seem to fall naturally into four areas: (1) sufficient dissatisfaction with the ways things are—enough frustration, discomfort, or pain; (2) a compelling vision of something new—an engaging sense of possibility, the pull of a better future;

(3) adequate energy to see the process through—knowing that change is usually not a sprint but a long-distance run; and (4) the discipline to mark the steps along the way.

As mentioned above, we must be skillful in our planning, but we must be open to the unexpected and hospitable to surprise. There is no excuse for careless planning, but we simply cannot muscle our plans into reality. The Mondragon worker-owner cooperatives in northern Spain offer a lively example. After forty years of astounding economic experimentation, seventeen machinists, who formed a single cooperative venture in 1954, have become 23,000 workers who own eighty-three economic units and embrace 45,000 family members that collectively have the highest per capita productivity in all of Spain. The cooperators say of this phenomenon, "We build the road as we go." They obviously have a clear vision and are rigorous in their goal setting and planning to build community based on what they call "equilibrio." Yet they have been astoundingly responsive and resilient, ready to find their way as the way has opened.[3]

## Action

God responded patiently to Moses for a time but then spoke boldly and clearly: "Moses, go!" And Moses did (Exodus 3:1—4:20). The angel Gabriel waited quietly until Mary quietly said, "Let it be with me according to your word" (Luke 1:38). Abraham knew precious little about the course or duration of the journey ahead, but beckoned by God's call, he faithfully left his home and the security of his walled city (Genesis 12:1-4). In several Gospel accounts, we read that each disciple, challenged to leave home, work, family, and security heard Jesus say, "Follow me," and did. A voice in the temple asked Isaiah a simple question, "Who will go for us?" He gave a simple answer, "Here I am, send me" (Isaiah 6:8). The ultimate goal of a visioning and planning process is action. Organizations, including churches, perhaps especially churches, are often more adept at conceiving bright ideas than taking concerted, effective action.

My first flight in a private plane lifted off from Montauk Point on Long Island, en route to Saranac Lake in upstate New York. I was fascinated by the broadening vistas of land and sea below us as we circled upward and headed across Long Island Sound. "Straight shot, Montauk Point to Saranac Lake, as the crow flies," I cheered.

"No, not exactly," explained the pilot as he penciled the first vectors of our flight plan on an aeronautical map. "Weather conditions, congestion over airports, changing terrain and wind drafts, and the flight patterns of other aircraft could alter our route several times. Air traffic controllers en route will instruct us about changes in our flight plan. In fact, unexpected weather conditions could force us to land at an airport short of our destination. We would have to wait for the weather to clear or rent a car and continue our trip by highway."

Two hours later, as we landed at the airport at Saranac Lake, I caught another glimpse of that aeronautical map. The lines on the map tracked our route precisely from takeoff to landing but formed anything but a straight line. We may have flown twice as many miles as the crow flies, and at some points we seemed to be flying away from our destination.

Destinations may be clear, but "flight plans" may change. The Promised Land. The kingdom of God. The ends of the earth. The destination must become clear and flight plans must be filed, but the ultimate route may take us on quite an adventure. Our job is to fasten our seat belts and prepare for take off!

The exodus narrative ends with a second water crossing story, less familiar than the first. Forty years earlier, Moses had parted the Red Sea waters with a raised shepherd's staff. By a "mighty hand and an outstretched arm" (Deuteronomy 26:8), the Hebrew nation passed through the waters to freedom. The waters parted, and they walked through. Now they stood at the edge of the Jordan, the long-anticipated Promised Land in sight across the river. Moses had spoken his parting words and then gone up onto the mountain to die. The Jordan waters were at flood stage. There was no outstretched arm or shepherd's staff. Joshua, their new leader, gave the instructions. He told them to gather at the edge of the water. He assured them that when the feet of the priests bearing the ark of the covenant touched the waters, the waters would part. The priests stepped forward, the waters parted, the way opened to their promised future, and the people followed.

The challenge before those of us who would envision and

empower a reinvented church is immense. We must find courage
to speak the truth in love, to name without flinching troubling and
discouraging realities, and to staunchly resist the hopelessness and
despair that is everywhere written on faces of congregational
leaders and church members. Simplistic answers are not answers
at all, and the promise of simple solutions proves hollow. The
change that is called for is radical and dramatic. It is inevitably
unsettling and even threatening. But I believe that congregations
and their leaders are awaiting someone to sound a call to rise to
meet this challenge.

This work must begin with recovering the sacred center of both
individuals and congregations. We must walk with steadiness,
patience, and hope. We must build and deepen community as we
walk together, nurturing temenos and kairos, sacred space and time,
an atmosphere of safety and trust. As leaders we must be ardently
committed to developing in ourselves character, competence, and
trustworthiness. We must be open to new ways of thinking and
venture onto new and uncharted pathways as new paradigm
pioneers. Unlike Harvey, we must break out of repetitious and
fruitless patterns. We must come to know our churches more
deeply and investigate fresh metaphors that might open up new
opportunities and point in new directions. We must build the
organizational life of the congregation from the inside out, discerning ways of living and working together in congregations
that are engaging and empowering. This work can be demanding,
discouraging, at times almost overwhelming. But above all, this
challenge will be ennobling and invigorating.

Let us envision with clarity and boldness and plan with diligence
and care. And then, let us stand together at the edge of the river and
walk!

# Building the Road as We Go

## A Case Study

By the spring of 1991 the rug in the community room of Gladwyne Presbyterian Church simply had to be replaced. The traffic patterns were obvious, and the rug's edges were fraying. The afternoon sun had coaxed out virtually all the color, and carelessly cleaned spills had left stains that made it look like a map of eastern Pennsylvania.

This was the rug on which we shed tears of joy and sadness, danced and played children's games, slept during work camps and youth group overnights, spilled coffee and ketchup and red wine. It was the rug where we planted our feet to hold a Bible on our knees and on which we knelt to pray. Called simply the social room, this was our "everything room"—the only space in the church other than the sanctuary that could hold more than a small circle of people.

We decided to have a party to say goodbye to the rug. We sat on the floor and shared a feast, pouring wine, eating like royalty, singing with gusto, and laughing heartily. We did not worry a bit about spilling.

We savored the banquet and then sat on the floor in a circle and began to tell "rug stories." The mood was playful at first, until memories awakened. People spoke with deep feeling and listened with unusual attentiveness. Several hours passed before all the stories had been told and we had finished our sharing. We ended the evening by pulling up the rug and cutting it into squares, one for each of us. My piece still hangs on my office wall.

Telling the stories of life, faithfulness, and ministry at Gladwyne Church takes me back to that evening. These stories—exciting, sometimes dramatic, and in many ways unlikely—may seem orderly and clear in the telling, but maybe only in retrospect can sense be made of them. Reality falls more neatly into place from a bird's eye view. Hindsight can see causes and effects, the intentions behind the realities. The fact is that our attempt to be faithful produced endless false starts, and we wandered endless dead-end streets.

Choosing to love and work together, we yet knew one another as a "mixed bag." Our commitment and follow-through were uneven, our attitude was not always the best, and we let each other down. We could become proud and arrogant. We discovered ourselves driven by guilt and do-goodism. We would argue ideology, our worldviews and viewpoints competing and colliding. Yet we managed to support and love one another, sometimes despite ourselves.

Often our best intentions, what we named as successes, we later viewed as flawed and imperfect, more hindering than helping. Groups from Trevor's Campaign fed hundreds of homeless on the streets of Philadelphia, only to realize they were fostering dependency and working at cross purposes with the more substantive work being done by other organizations. A mission group traveled to Mexico and constructed badly needed roofs on shacks of families they had met in La Estacion, a squatters' settlement in the railroad yard in Cuernavaca, only to find that they had stirred resentment among the families not chosen and fractured a fragile spirit of cooperation that had been growing in that community.

This is one congregation's outreach story. It is about people—everyday folks who were stirred, saddened, outraged, and inspired; who were awakened, converted, and empowered. This is a story about real people with real names. Indeed, the credits would run longer than the film.

The Bible did not have chapters and verses until the invention of moveable type, when a printer with a yen for order and structure created them. History, intrinsically, has no eras until a historian invents them. Real events transpire in time and space, but their meaning is abstract. So these eras in the Gladwyne story are convenient but highly contrived. Let me open a window or two on this twenty-three-year time line so you can glimpse and overhear something of the story.

## A Hesitant Start

I arrived at Gladwyne Church in 1970 with activist credentials. I marched for civil rights in Roosevelt, New York, spoke early and vigorously against the war in Vietnam, and helped convene a team of people in Montauk Community Church who sponsored a ten-week summer work-study program for inner-city youth from Harlem. I organized a group of young adults to form a tutoring program for local high school youth, joined a coalition of religious leaders in Suffolk County, New York, who met with Cesar Chavez to organize potato field workers, worked with an ecumenical council in nearby East Hampton to plan youth work camps to do home improvement with what we came to call the "invisible population," those who lived in tar paper shacks down dirt roads that wound behind the elegant homes. I organized a confrontation with real estate agents in Montauk whom we had proven discriminated against black Air Force personnel from the radar station located in our town. Whatever my goal, however, my style was always to work collaboratively with members and friends of the church. The committee that hired me at Gladwyne was aware of this dimension of my ministry.

In the early months, my calls to social justice and personal involvement in ministries of compassion and service seemed to fall on deaf ears. There was some active resistance but mostly disinterest. I felt frustrated but determined.

In the spring of 1971, Bryan, a university professor, cornered some folks at a coffee hour after church and suggested that they start a book discussion group. The first meeting, held in his home, drew a circle of five. They decided to continue, rotating the meetings among their homes, and by fall their numbers swelled to a steady dozen.

George, a member of the group with affection for Quaker spirituality and social concern, suggested at the September meeting, "Let's go on a Quaker work camp to West Philadelphia." They chose a date, made some posters, and put up a sign-up sheet. To everyone's surprise, they recruited nineteen people.

A veteran work camp leader welcomed our group. Everyone looked hesitant and anxious. We had come to one of Philadelphia's most economically depressed communities, where the crime rate was high. He briefed us on the protocols of the neighborhood and the ground rules we were to follow. The group was very attentive and ready to be very observant!

Deployed in teams of four to six, we fanned out to different work locations. A group of three cleaned out the attic of an eighty-six-year-old widow confined to a wheelchair. Another team replaced drywall that an abusive husband had trashed in a rage two weeks before. A contingent cleared a corner lot so a neighborhood garden could be planted, finding syringes and drug paraphernalia scattered amid the trash and broken bottles. Four more went grocery shopping for a thirty-three-year-old mother who could not leave the bedside of her seventeen-year-old-son, who had been shot in a gang clash three weeks earlier.

Beyond the impact of that work camp on nineteen people, these forty-five hours were to have a profound effect on the life of the church at large. The experience did not end with the circle of Quaker-style silence at three o'clock on Sunday afternoon. A twenty-three-year momentum began that day.

Tye, a young printing salesman, was barely home an hour when he began to call folks from the church to join him. Every Saturday morning, teams of six to ten people would head to Germantown, another depressed neighborhood in Philadelphia, to do winterizing projects at homes of the elderly. Morry, a teacher at Montgomery County Community College, convened a group of people to visit inmates at Gratersford Prison, a medium-security facility about twenty miles from Gladwyne. Aldina and Joyce, housewives and mothers of small children, gathered a group of five or six women who carpooled on Wednesday mornings to work with teachers and students at an elementary school in an inner-city neighborhood. Something had come alive at the church.

## Partnerships Form

Russell, a black pastor from a neighborhood where the church sponsored a project that had grown out of the work camp experience seven years earlier, spoke one evening at a church supper. We guessed he would be glowing with affirmation and appreciation. He did express his gratitude but then confronted us with a probing observation. "Mothers in my neighborhood send their children to school an hour early so they can catch a train to the Bryn Mawr station," he began in a quiet and even tone, "where mothers from Gladwyne pick them up and bring them to the house, where they'll work all day to clean and prepare dinner. The Gladwyne mothers then carpool back to my neighborhood to tutor the children of those mothers who are busy cleaning and cooking. Something about that doesn't make sense to me," he concluded. We felt too self-conscious to say much, but we heard his words all too clearly.

Bill and Kay, new members who arrived at the church with a long history of involvement in social issues, had sampled two different service projects sponsored by the church but found neither to their liking. "Something is missing," they said, "but we're not sure what it is." They listened intently as Russell issued his challenge.

"We think we know what the problem is," they confided when I was making a pastoral visit. "We don't have a relationship with the people we work with. We arrive on a Saturday, work in their homes for the day, share a bag lunch or a glass of iced tea, but a week later we've forgotten their names. How can we establish deeper connection with these people?" Bill and Kay were not complaining. They were searching. And they were not just talkers. They were doers. Two weeks later, with four or five others from the church who shared their concern, they drove to our denomination's regional office in downtown Philadelphia to meet with a staff person who coordinated inner-city ministry.

"Go and see Cordell Sloane at Temple Church in the Ludlow neighborhood," was the executive's immediate reply. The meeting that day was short, but visits to Ludlow continue today. Families from Gladwyne linked with families from Ludlow. "Prepositions can make all the difference," Kay commented one afternoon, working with a team of mothers from Gladwyne and mothers from Ludlow in what came to be called Tuesday School. "We used to come and work *for* Ludlow, but now we come to work *with* Ludlow."

Tuesday School recently had its eighteenth anniversary. A partnership between Marvin Louis, the mayor of Ludlow, and George and Linda's team has touched twenty-five households. The Ludlow Drywall Company and the Ludlow Cooperative Bakery were short-lived, but those failures were celebrated too. And partnership had become a value for outreach ministry at Gladwyne Church.

## Reverse Mission: a Quantum Leap

Jeff was a guitarist and lead singer in a rock band, and with floppy hair and just the right glasses he really did look a lot like John Denver. When I met him, he convinced me immediately that he was the right choice to be our youth minister. Some called the decade that followed the "Jeff Singleton era," a most appropriate title. Jeff became a one-man revolution on the youth and outreach ministry front. He was the right person at the right time to beckon the church forward in the next steps in ministry of compassion and service.

Jeff wasted no time encouraging innovation. The Outreach Associates were formed, a team of teenagers who visited every nearby organization that received financial support from the church's benevolence budget, gave them personal encouragement, then interpreted their work to the congregation. The Outreach Travel Service provided any church member willing to include a mission site visit in their vacation plans with a detailed itinerary and a $200 check to deliver.

### Trevor's Story

December 6, 1983, was Pearl Harbor Day, but it became a date to remember for a different reason at Gladwyne Church. That evening eleven-year-old Trevor Ferrell, a fifth grader in our Sunday school, gave a pillow and a blanket to a man on a sidewalk vent.

An early snowfall had coated the city streets, and the nighttime temperature was hovering near zero. The six o'clock news showed a middle-aged man huddled under a cardboard box on a center city heat vent. "He's doesn't live there, does he?" Trevor asked his mom.

"Yes, he does," his mother replied, wishing she had changed the channel.

"But that can't be," Trevor protested.

"Yes, son," his father chimed in, "it's true."

"No, no, it just can't be," Trevor pleaded.

"Put on your jacket and bring your pillow and blanket, Trevor," his father said, getting up from his chair. "I'll start the car and warm it up, and then we'll drive downtown so I can show you." Trevor tucked himself in the backseat, his mother hopped in the passenger side, and they headed for the expressway and the fifteen-minute ride to center city. They stopped for a red light, and Trevor spotted a man on a vent, just like he had seen on the news. His mother hastily pushed down the lock button on her door, and his father revved the engine awaiting the green light—while Trevor slipped out the back door, dragging his pillow and blanket!

"Trevor!" his mother yelled, but he was across the street out of earshot. The youngster approached the man on the vent hesitantly, leaned down, and quietly said, "Excuse me, mister, but would you like a pillow and a blanket?" The man looked up. "I sure would," he said. "And God bless you."

"God bless you too," Trevor replied, and walked back to the car.

I heard that story a week later. I was walking past the TV repair shop where Trevor's father worked. Just below the "Ferrell's TV Repair" sign was a smaller, hand-lettered sign: "Wanted— blankets for the homeless." Frank saw me and beckoned me inside. He told me the story of the pillow and the blanket then went on to say that Trevor was now collecting blankets to make another trip, and that he had asked his mother if they could make a Crock-Pot of hamburger stew to serve to the homeless who gathered near the vent where they had stopped before. "Could we say something about this in church next Sunday, Howard?" Frank asked.

"Sure," I said, finding his enthusiasm contagious.

That next Sunday night three church members joined the Ferrell family in their twelve-passenger van, the aroma of franks and beans, tuna casserole, and meat loaf wafting from Crock-Pots and aluminum casserole tins packed in the back of the van next to an urn of hot coffee. We had no idea this was the first of a thousand consecutive nights of serving food and distributing blankets, gloves, and sweaters on what came to be called the "Trevor Food Run."

Three months later the church was given the deed to a thirty-three room abandoned boarding house in North Philadelphia, which was slowly renovated by teams of volunteers. As soon as the old heating system was coaxed back to life, the first residents moved in— Chico, Big Al, Cornelius, and Ralph. Some of the people who lived on the vents asked if they could come to church, so the van began

a Sunday-morning circuit to our regular food stops. Parishioners
found it harder than they expected to slip into a pew with someone
who had obviously slept, perhaps for several nights, in the clothes
they were wearing. Ralph had never been baptized; he asked
Harriet, an elder of the church, to be his godmother and was
baptized one April Sunday. Dennis and Linda were a homeless
couple, and they had never been married. One Sunday in early June
the "Wedding March" replaced the closing hymn, as Linda, in a
donated wedding dress, and Dennis, in a borrowed tuxedo, marched
down the aisle. Our associate minister performed the service and
led them in exchanging their vows. Chico had never seen a rod and
reel up close, so Len took him bay fishing at the Jersey shore.

The impact on the church and its members reached well beyond
opportunities to participate in Trevor's Campaign. Following
Trevor's example, people realized that the step from seeing and
caring to acting was shorter and easier than they thought. If an
attitude shift is a key to change, the groundwork was laid for an
exciting future.

There was more to come in this amazing church year. We called
Nena out of retirement to become our part-time adult education staff
person. Whereas Jeff was colorful, animated, unpredictable, and
outlandish, Nena was quiet, understated, patient, and steady. She
asked good questions and listened to people intently. She was an
enabler and encourager. She affirmed and reassured people.

Nena had long appreciated a Christian congregation in Washington, D.C., called Church of the Saviour. Gordon Cosby, an ordained
Baptist minister, began Church of the Saviour in 1945, when he was
discharged from the chaplain corps. He wanted to see if his somewhat unorthodox approach to ministry, which had been appreciated
at military bases where he had served, might take hold in a new
church development. The amazing story of this network of eight
worshiping and serving communities has been widely documented.

Nena had a dream of taking a delegation from Gladwyne to what
Church of the Saviour calls a Wellspring Orientation, a three-day
event held at their retreat center in the rolling hills of eastern
Maryland that invites participants to thirty-six hours of what they
call the Inward Journey—a time of silence, reflection, and quiet
sharing, followed by thirty-six hours of Outward Journey—travel-
ling to various locations in downtown Washington where teams of

church members, who call themselves mission groups, carry out a rather astounding array of ministries.

To Nena's delight the opportunity came and twelve members of Gladwyne Church, an even mix of men and women including both a retired teacher and a group of four teenagers, were able to attend. Five years later a delegate from that group, aware of what a profound impact those three days had on both the participants and the church at large, commented, "Our group was large enough to become leaven in the life of the church when we got back. And Howard didn't go."

That woman was right, I think, on both counts. This group became a critical mass and changed our congregation. When they came home from the weekend, they returned to their respective Bible study, women's, men's, single mothers' and youth groups speaking a new language, sharing a fresh approach, glowing with a new energy, and offering a new vision. The spirit was contagious. And this venture had not been my idea. It belonged to the people. I felt, to be honest, quietly threatened. A part of me was delighted, and I gave voice to that. But a part of me, frankly, was a bit undone. The reality of lay empowerment was more difficult than I anticipated.

It was during these years that understanding and experience of what we would come to call the recovering of the sacred center began to be born. People at the church began to read and appreciate contemplative devotional literature. "Inward journeying" became a familiar and generative phrase, describing a commitment and personal discipline, as well as a concept. Prayerfulness became a cornerstone of personal and congregational decision making.

## An Outreach Explosion

It seems difficult to name the moment when the match was put to the fuse that ignited the explosion. Among the possibilities, this story seems as likely as any.

It was August 1985. I flew into Port au Prince, Haiti, on Monday afternoon, two days after our youth delegation arrived. Betsy and I yielded to a last-minute urging and joined the group, as participants not leaders. A team from Ministry of Money, a mission group from Church of the Saviour, led the group. Trevor (another Trevor) and Linda rode with Mike, our leader, in an old pickup truck to meet me at the airport. En route to where we were staying, they took me on a tour of the places the group had visited over the past forty-eight hours.

We bounced downtown along one of the city's better roads, pocked with craterlike ruts and potholes and thick with gaily painted public transports called "tap-taps," pickup trucks rigged with bench seats, surrounded by pipe railings, and covered with a canopy. Suddenly a circle of people along the side of the road caught our attention. The body of a young man, stained with blood where a bullet had entered, lay lifeless in the gutter. This would become a familiar sight, but I was not ready.

We came to the Iron Market, a center-city shopping area adjacent to the wharf, where we parked the truck and walked for several blocks. I have never stood, before or since, on a more thickly populated street. "Hey mister," a little boy no more than seven said, in hesitant but practiced English, "You want a woman? Do anything you want. Cheap." He nodded toward his sister standing nearby. She could not have been more than thirteen. I hastened my pace back toward the truck.

Our tour brought us finally to Cité Soleil, a shanty town of shacks I had spotted from the plane as we made our approach to the airport. We parked the truck and pressed our way along narrow passage-ways that wound haphazardly and were lined with shacks crafted of bedsprings, cardboard, packing crates, and pieces of billboard, with strands of rusty wire weaving it all together. Our little contingent wended its way to an "intersection"—a rare open space, where a familiar U.S.-style street post stood incongru-ously, holding at right angles two green street signs that read "Boston" and "Brooklyn."

We were standing in the middle of what Mother Teresa called the poorest neighborhood on the face of the planet. If I were to create in my mind's eye a movie set intended to depict the most awful and awesome of poverty, I could do no better than this. The heat was suffocating. Two little boys made motor boat sounds as they pushed scraps of wood along a rivulet of water. A glance at the water, or a whiff of it, told me where the water came from.

Then, in a scene indelibly etched in my memory, I watched a naked little boy edge his way out onto a tiny pond of water. He tried to walk on tiny rocks or pieces of wood to keep his feet dry, inching toward an orange peel, which he finally grasped between his thin little fingers and from which he tried to suck a last drop of juice. The "pond" was the accumulating local sewage not yet absorbed by the scorching noonday sun. Mercifully, a tug on my arm by two little girls broke my concentration. They sat me down on a broken crate, fascinated by my white hair, which was a bit longer that summer, and commenced to plait its strands in endless braids.

We walked to the truck in silence and looked out the windows with vacant stares as we rode back to the center. I understood only vaguely the concept of "psychic numbing"—until that visit to Cité Soleil. We drove through the gates to our compound, and I jumped from the back of the pickup dazed and disoriented.

## Naming Locations: Another Lens

Mission trips became the launching pad for a growing outreach ministry involving a rapidly increasing number of people. Partnership became the norm. A mission trip could involve a five-hour flight to Cuernavaca, Mexico, or a half-hour drive to the center of Philadelphia, but each became the springboard.

### Haiti: Poorest Nation in the Western Hemisphere

Rivers and streams from the headwaters of the 1985 Haiti mission trip flow in every direction. Of the nine youth who made that pilgrimage ten years ago, John is completing an internship in tropical disease, preparing for a career in third-world medicine. Linda, after serving for five years as a lay missionary in Mexico, is doing Ph.D. studies in third-world politics. Erik develops small businesses in Mexico, providing training and financing that allows workers, who would otherwise be underemployed at the $3.50-per-day minimum wage, to become worker-owners. David recently completed a Ph.D. degree in sociology and teaches with a commitment to foster social consciousness in his students. Heather is a medical technologist working in an inner-city hospital in Philadelphia. David recently completed a double stint in the Peace Corps in Africa.

Steve went to Haiti and now collects soap scraps from area hotels and ships them to Port au Prince in hundred-pound lots, knowing that in a home in Cité Soleil, a cake of soap can be the difference between cleaning a simple abrasion and dying from its infection.

Sara went to Haiti and started a small scholarship fund of $100-per-year donors, knowing that each contribution educates an elementary age child for a year. That fund recently passed the $5,000 mark. Iain, the chief of medicine of a prominent children's hospital in Philadelphia, maintains contact with pediatricians in Port au Prince, ships medical supplies and equipment, and has arranged for medical interns to spend a rotation at the Schweitzer Hospital in the Haitian back country. Dray and Carol went to Haiti and remain in steady contact with Father Roger Desir, a Haitian-born Episcopal priest, welcoming him to their home for periodic R and R, and raising $35,000 for his work there. Sixteen people from Gladwyne Church have made at least one trip to Haiti, and most maintain an ongoing involvement.

## Nicaragua: Befriending the Enemy

In February 1986, Erik, a seventeen-year-old high school junior, joined a fact-finding and orientation tour to Nicaragua. Particularly impressed by the Agricultural Mechanization School near Esteli, he vowed as he waved goodbye to the students that he would return that summer with a team of high school volunteers. Somehow, he convinced the reluctant parents of nine youth group members to allow them to make the trip.

One afternoon, after a hard day's work at the construction site, the weary group walked to a nearby village to buy sodas. As dusk approached they decided to head back, passing a contingent of Sandinista soldiers climbing out of the back of a transport truck at the edge of the village. A few of the teens were studying Spanish, and this was a chance to practice. Guessing that they were about to walk back to the mechanization school, a young Nicaraguan called a warning, "Este está una idea mala" ("that is a bad idea"). In daylight, they explained, the Contras, the enemies of the Sandinistas, could clearly see the difference between a Nicaraguan and an Anglo, but not at night. (Congress had recently voted an additional aid package to support the Contra effort, and the Sandinistas were clearly named as enemies, according to official U.S. foreign policy.)

A half hour later those teens found themselves climbing into the back of a truck packed with soldiers, bouncing along the gravel road back home. "I smiled as I thought to myself," reminisced one of the group, "here we are riding with the 'enemy,' who are protecting us from our 'allies'!" The teenagers finished their month-long commitment and still proudly show pictures of themselves standing beside a completed two-story brick building on the Mechanization School campus.

Over the next four years, two other delegations journeyed to Nicaragua, and a partnership ministry grew. Neal and Jeff, working with the youth group, gathered, repaired, and shipped 750 bicycles to the University of Central America in Managua, to be used by students who have no other means of transportation. Money was raised to build twelve kilometers of bike paths as well as a small warehouse on the edge of the campus to store and repair bicycles. Pat, an audiovisual technician, went to Nicaragua to make a video telling what she viewed as the untold story of that country, then sent it with a cover letter to eighty-seven Congress members viewed as swing votes in a Contra-aid debate, as well as thirty-five public television stations across the country. David, a longtime Central American activist, raises money to support the music ministry of a Christian family in Managua and a furniture-making workshop for soldiers disabled in the war.

## Cuernavaca: La Lucha Compartida ("The Shared Struggle")

It was November 1986. Betsy and I had gone to Mexico to pick up our son after he had attended six weeks of language school in Cuernavaca. Rather serendipitously we met Ray Plankey, director of a center that brings Mexicans and North Americans together for dialogue. He invited us for breakfast and gave us an orientation to his work. We were impressed, and when we got home, we hastily prepared a brochure, distributed it at the church, and convinced nine people to join us for what we called "Sun and Service," five days of service in Cuernavaca, then four of sun in Cancun.

In the years since, ten mission delegations have journeyed to Cuernavaca. Each group begins with home stays, a weekend in a small community staying in pairs in the homes of peasants, working with the villagers on community projects, and sharing in a Sunday afternoon fiesta. During the nine-day experience the delegates visit the homes of Salvadoran and Guatemalan refugees, learn of the work of the Christian base communities and other justice-seeking projects, and have time to reflect personally, and then to share their thoughts and feelings with each other. Participants have often called their experience a "second conversion."

Delle went to Mexico, then returned to leave her career as an actress, sell her spacious suburban home, and enroll as a seminary student. She now lives in Cuernavaca, works with Artisanos Unidos, an artisans' cooperative, and is codirector of the center where our groups stay. Trip grads Judy, John, and Pat market artisan crafts through sales at local churches, earning $3,000 each year in proceeds from sales at Gladwyne. Frank, Priscilla, and Peter felt drawn to the work of a community-based housing group called Colonos Pobladores Citlatcali, modeled after Habitat for Humanity. This trio offers technical and hands-on assistance and has raised $25,000 at the church for the project. Morris has not been to Cuernavaca but has provided a revolving loan fund for shop owners in a small community produce market. Erik continues his effort to develop worker-owner cooperatives.

## Chester: The Port au Prince of Pennsylvania

Many participants, after a mission trip experience, maintain a connection to the people and projects they encountered on their pilgrimage and find ways to continue a long-distance ministry. But the majority find their mission field closer to home. Sara went to Haiti and continues to maintain an active tie to the friends she has made there.

Eight years ago she was hired as a horticulturalist by Penn State Urban Gardening and assigned to Chester, Pennsylvania, about forty-five minutes from her home. She had every reason to complain or simply to be frightened. Only East St. Louis is a poorer city of similar size in the United States. The statistics of poverty are too unsettling to list. She could have called it bad luck. She calls it grace.

For five years Sara led weekly contingents of Gladwyne members to Chester to work in raised-bed, high-yield vegetable gardening. She convened a Thursday morning Bible study group that brought suburban whites and Chester blacks together and became the lifeblood of a partnership ministry. She helped to nurture a grassroots, neighborhood-based organization called Community Togetherness that links Chester citizens and congregations with their counterparts in suburban communities.

Brian, a high school teacher and songwriter-musician, worked

with Chester community leaders to form Learn and Earn, a tutoring
and work skills development program for potential high school
dropouts. Pat, who works with learning disabled preschool children, participates in a program designed to enhance parenting skills
for young mothers. Elaine, Julie, Don, and Jeff formed a team from
Gladwyne Church to work with community leaders to organize an
eight-week day camp for 130 children, which also provided em-
ployment for twenty-three teen counselors.

### Here, There, and Everywhere

Barbara was walking one day past the park at Independence Hall
in Philadelphia, and a circle of people standing by an open hole and
unplanted tree caught her eye. Chief Jake Swamp, of the Akwasasne
Tribe of the Iroquois Nation and Mohawk Confederacy, was leading a peace tree planting ceremony. Barb wandered close enough
to hear the chief's words and was deeply touched. She chatted with
him after the crowd had dispersed and invited him to the church.
One Sunday the chief shared the traditional stories of his tribe with
the congregation. Worshipers were amazed by the fascinating parallels to the foundational biblical stories. A group of people felt
drawn to the needs of the tribe and formed a mission group to
respond.

Bill completed his master's degree in school administration and
became the principal of a multiracial, multiethnic middle school in
the Philadelphia school district. His wife, Penny, was an early
childhood specialist and worked with the district's Head Start
program. "A mission trip can mean an airline ticket to Mexico or
Haiti, or a bus or trolley token to the city," they announced in church
one Sunday. They handed out a colorful little brochure they had
prepared that featured the public transportation system, with instructions for a mission trip to Olney where Bill's school was
located, or Overbrook where Penny worked. Soon teams of three
or four, some riding a trolley or city bus for the very first time, were
working as volunteers with Bill or Penny in both in-school and
after-school programs.

Anne and Wayne and their three daughters, regular worshipers
at Gladwyne Church and active in church program, chose to continue to live in the city. Their neighborhood was undergoing
changes that cause most white families to move to the suburbs. They

stayed. Teachers in city schools and active in neighborhood organizations, they were keenly aware of the many needs of inner-city students and the resources of suburbs like Gladwyne. They were aware as well of a vitality, resilience, and spirit that city kids had to offer suburban folks. They initiated a youth group exchange. They sponsored sports events to bring the two communities together. Rather spontaneously, a Bible study group started with Haitian-born teens in West Philadelphia and teens and adults from Gladwyne. It became "reverse mission" of the first order.

Reaching out is a spirit. It may express itself visibly in a variety of programs and projects sponsored by the church. But it may also express itself quietly and unofficially, privately and independently. Many members find ways to serve and carry them out informally and personally.

## Naming the Principles

I have presented most of this conclusion as story. All of this work unfolded in its own way and in its own time. To be sure, goals were set, plans were made, teams were formed, and tasks were carried out. Yet the winds of the Spirit blew in and through it all. Rabbi Gamaliel, quoted in the Book of Acts, reminds us that whatever is of God will not be stopped (5:34-39). We celebrate the hand of God at work in this story, and we know that much that we plotted and schemed failed.

These stories truly had a life of their own, emerging from some inner dynamic. But a group of us were reminiscing one afternoon near the end of my tenure at Gladwyne Church, wondering if there were basic principles at work, woven through these stories. One of us took notes as we chatted. These ten principles, discerned largely in retrospect, were the result of our reflection.

### 1. Journey Inward / Journey Outward / In Community

Though clearly resonating with the life and work of Church of the Saviour in Washington, we came to this threefold principle through our own process. If you asked any member of the Gladwyne congregation what were the core principles of the church, they would likely offer a version of this formula:

*Inward Journeying.* We call individuals and groups within the church to a disciplined spiritual life that may include reflection on

Scripture, prayer, silence and stillness, spiritual reading, journaling, and so forth. We recognize that people with busy lives must set aside and protect such time.

*Outward Journeying.* We believe all are called to witness to and embody the Christian message in the world. We believe each person is uniquely called and gifted for a particular ministry. We invite and encourage one another to discern that call and then follow it with faithfulness—individually or with others who shared that call.

*In Community.* We believe that only with the nurturing of community are we free to be open and vulnerable to the Word of God and its challenge.

Some in the church found the mystical/contemplative theological tradition to be a bridge, a theological base that avoids polarization between prayerfulness and action, indeed that grounds social justice ministry in a spiritual rooting. This tradition invites believers to an ever deeper and richer prayer life yet embraces a call to make love visible in the world. Some liked to call themselves "contemplative activists."

## 2. Be in, but Not of the World

The challenge to the church and its members, we believed, is to live as strangers and sojourners in the world, to be creatively out of step with the culture's values, to be faithfully countercultural. We sought to be citizens first of the kingdom of God, to seek that kingdom's claim as highest priority, and only then to be citizens of our country. We sought to be loving critics, or "critical lovers," of nation and culture. Borrowing from the methodology of liberation theology and Christian base communities, we felt called to critical analysis of culture, the world, and unfolding history—seeking to discern where God is at work in the culture, the world, and history—and then to join that work. And we were not unaware that the culture constantly seeks to capture and domesticate the church itself.

## 3. Protect the Dialogue, Affirm the Dialectic

We encouraged vigorous dialogue and debate, a crisp expression and exchange of ideas, ideologies, and various positions on theological and social issues. We came to embrace Hegel's principle of the dialectic—a process that encourages vigorous expression of thesis, then antithesis, so that synthesis, a still higher and more complete truth, might be discerned. This deeply held belief allowed hearty interaction among people, each speaking and listening with high respect. This principle seemed to free us to address difficult theological and social issues without undue polarization. We adopted a policy that the church as a whole would not take public positions on issues, though individuals and groups within the church were encouraged to do so.

It was not uncommon at a coffee hour for members to circulate petitions on opposite sides of a given issue. The challenge was not to take the "right" position on an issue, but rather to address the issue forthrightly, to seek the light of Scripture, to reflect patiently and prayerfully, and then, if a position became clear, to advocate for it.

## 4. High-Touch, Hands-On Mission

For many years, "mission" had meant to us sending checks to benevolence budget recipients. Only occasionally did members make gestures of personal involvement. The percentage of the annual budget designated for missions was meager, and outside-the-budget giving was virtually nonexistent. When the church began to challenge members to discern their personal call to involvement in mission and to offer substantive guidance in follow-through, an "outreach revolution" broke out. At one point this church of 325 members had eighteen different mission groups with as few as three and as many as twelve members. Mission giving rose to just over 50 percent of the annual budget, including $95,000 in successive years raised for outside-the-budget gifts.

## 5. Discernment, Then Decision Making and Planning

The individual and corporate commitment to discernment broadened and deepened across the years. There was a constant quest for clearer definition of this process, though intuition often eludes reason and management. What would God have us be doing? Where is your heart leading you? How is God calling and gifting you for serving at this time? Which way would the winds of the Spirit send us? We tried to keep these kinds of questions continually before us and to remain alert and open to God's leading. And when "the way openeth," as the Quakers say, we tried to follow it. We

were well into this journey together when we began to name this
commitment as recovering the sacred center.

## 6. The "Blank Check" Principle

A comment I frequently hear in my consulting practice, typically
from the finance and budget committee, is, "That's a great idea, but
it's not in the budget."

"Do you have the money?" I quickly ask.

The answer is rarely no. "Oh, we have the money," comes the
usual reply, "but it's not in the budget."

"If you have the money, why not vote to allocate it?" I offer as
a logical response.

"But it's not in the budget," comes the incessant reply.

At Gladwyne Church we made two decisions. The first was that
we would spend money if we had it, whether it was in the budget
or not. That did make the financial types uneasy, so we made a
second decision. At the beginning of each year we set aside as much
as 33 percent of the overall budget as undesignated. A portion
became benevolence commitment, so those who came forward
during the church year with new ideas for outreach ministry could
apply for a grant, as if this set-aside money were an internal
foundation. And a portion was designed to support church programs, so those with new program ideas could apply for financial
support to get them started. This may have been as important a
single strategic decision as we ever made. It immediately affirmed
and empowered initiative from the laity.

## 7. Faithfulness, Not Success

The freedom to risk must be linked to the freedom to fail.
Because I am an avid lover of *Zorba the Greek*, scenes and images
from that book and movie were familiar to the congregation through
my preaching. Zorba and his young friend had a scheme, a way to
bring logs down from the top of a mountain and thus to get rich.
There is a scene in which the huge, complicated, awkward structure
they had built creaks, cracks, and then crumbles in a thunderous
and complete collapse. Zorba and his young friend had put their
time, their hearts, and all their money into this unlikely project.
They are broke! The air is filled with the sound of crashing lumber,
and dust swirls around them. You can see their shadows, but you

cannot yet see their faces. Then you hear Zorba begin to laugh, a deep, hearty laugh. You can see him clearly now as his head flies back and his body seems to dance the laughter.

Though often difficult, we chose to laugh in the face of failure, to dance with disappointment as well as with delight, to celebrate commitment, hard work, and loyalty, whether we were successful or not.

## 8. The Partnership Principle

Years ago we made it a policy to distribute among those who worked in mission and outreach ministry an article by Father Albert Nolan titled "Stages of Spiritual Growth in Helping the Poor."[1] Nolan suggests that working with the poor begins with compassion, but that is only a starting point. Although love and caring must be at the heart of this ministry and what leads us to action, they can foster an attitude that obscures the call to justice.

Nolan's second stage is the discovery that poverty is a structural problem, that it is institutionalized and systemic. The poor, thus the nonpoor as well, are pawns in an unjust system. Compassion must be tempered and shaped by political awareness.

Nolan's third stage, which sounds at first to be harsh and abrupt, is the discovery that the poor must save themselves and that we cannot and must not even attempt to do it for them. Problems must be solved and structures must be changed, but "we" cannot do it for "them." Paolo Freire, a Brazilian educator who has been highly influential in liberation theology and the Christian base community movement, argues that only the oppressed can free the oppressor. The fourth stage, which seems at first hearing cynical and depressing, is the disillusionment of finding that the poor commit sins, make mistakes, and sometimes spoil their own cause. Our romanticized vision of the poor shatters.

If Nolan is right, and my experience suggests that he is, then this hard news is also good news. If we persist through these stages, true partnership, solidarity, and deep mutuality become possibilities.

## 9. The Reverse Mission Principle

Gwen participated in a Mexico mission trip seven years ago. At a follow-up gathering some weeks after our ten days in Cuernavaca, she commented, "I thought my airline ticket to Mexico was the mission trip ticket, but I've come to discover that the mission trip took place when I used the ticket home. I went to teach them, help them, serve them, and love them, and I suppose I did, but not nearly as deeply as they taught, helped, served, and loved me." Another participant in the circle chimed in, "Someone at the church asked me, rather cynically I thought, why I didn't stay at home and send the $750 to Cuernavaca to help the poor. I don't think he understood my response, but I told him that, as it turned out, the trip wasn't for the poor in Mexico. It was for me in Gladwyne."

## 10. Not My Will, but Yours Be Done

To dare to discern a call to outreach ministry, to strive to faithfully make caring and love visible and concrete in the world, to undertake a project you believe to answer God's call, can be humbling. Vulnerability and failure are constant intruders. Frustration and discouragement seem forever at hand. The disinterested and uninvolved often seem more prudent. These, perhaps, are much needed antidotes for arrogance and paternalism. Both parts of Jesus' prayers in the garden seem helpful. In the first part of his prayer, as I read it, Jesus outlined his plan to God—to let the cup pass, to escape the moment, to extend his years of ministry. Only then did he pray the more familiar part—"not my will, but yours be done" (Luke 22:42).

## In Closing

Did these twenty-plus years of outreach make any difference? Is the world a better place for our efforts? Is there any discernible impact? Though it was difficult to do, we came to resist and distrust those questions. Paraphrasing Reinhold Niebuhr, we worked diligently for penultimate goals, as we set them and ardently pursued them. The ultimate goals are up to God. Like the author of that unknown prayer, we prayed as if it were all up to God and worked as if it were all up to us.

# Notes

## Part One

1. Marshall Berman, *All That Is Solid Melts into Air: The Experience of Modernity* (New York: Penguin Books, 1988), 6.

## Chapter One

1. Joel Arthur Barker, *Paradigms: The Business of Discovering the Future* (New York: Harper Business, 1993), 71-83.

2. Thomas Merton, *New Seeds of Contemplation* (New York: New Directions Books, 1963), especially 21-36, 64-69, 268-274.

3. Walter Brueggemann, "The Transformative Agenda of the Pastoral Office," an audiocassette of a lecture on February 25, 1984. See also Walter Brueggemann, *The Prophetic Imagination* (Philadelphia: Fortress Press, 1978), 109-113.

4. J. Robert Oppenheimer, "Prospects in the Arts and Sciences," in *Uncommon Sense*, N. Metropolis, et al., eds. (Boston: Birkhauser, 1984), 84.

5. Edwin A. Abbott, *Flatland: A Romance of Many Dimensions* (New York: Signet Classic Books, 1984).

6. George Barna, in a lecture and discussion at Eastern Baptist Theological Seminary, April 26, 1996.

7. Marvin R. Weisbord, *Discovering Common Ground* (San Francisco: Berrett-Koehler, 1992), 101-103.

## Chapter Two

1. Rainer Maria Rilke, *Letters to a Young Poet*, trans. Stephen R. Mitchell (New York: Vintage Books, 1984), 34.

2. T. S. Eliot, *Four Quartets* (New York: Harcourt Brace and Company, 1971), 59.

3. Morris West, *Shoes of the Fisherman* (New York: St. Martin's Press, 1991).

4. The *Collected Works of St. Teresa of Avila*, vol. 2, trans. Kieran Kavenaugh and Otilio Rodriguez (Washington, D.C.: Institute of Carmelite Studies, 1980), 268.

5. Ibid., summarized from 281-452.

6. *The Collected Works of St. John of the Cross*, trans. Kieran Kavenaugh and Otilio Rodriguez (Washington, D.C.: Institute of Carmelite Studies, 1979), 15-37.

7. Quoted from a lecture by Richard Shaull, "Christian Witness in a Secular World," Princeton Theological Seminary, October 18, 1963. See also Dietrich Bonhoeffer, *Christ the Center* (New York: Harper and Row, 1960), 66-67, 106-110.

8. Thomas Merton, "The Inner Experience: Notes on Contemplation" (unpublished), 6, quoted in Thomas Findlay, *Merton's Palace of Nowhere: A Search for God Through Awareness of the True Self* (Notre Dame, Ind.: Ave Maria Press, 1978), 87.

9. *The Cloud of Unknowing* (anon.), ed. William Johnson (New York: Doubleday, 1973), 57-64.

10. Gerald May, *Will and Spirit* (San Francisco: Harper and Row, 1982), 6, 13, 27.

## Chapter Three

1. Italo Calvino, "Cybernetics and Ghosts," in Italo Calvino, *The Uses of Literature* (New York: Harcourt, Brace, Jovanovich, 1982), 18.

2. The language and table metaphor builds on the work of Paul vanBuren, from a lecture presentation and discussion at a Young Pastors' Conference, October 28-29, 1971, at Princeton Theological Seminary. See also Paul vanBuren, *The Secular Meaning of the Gospel* (New York: Macmillan, 1963), 81-108.

## Chapter Four

1. Ernest Gordon, *Through the Valley of the Kwai* (New York: Harper and Row, 1962).

2. David Steindl-Rast, *Gratefulness: The Heart of Prayer* (New York: Paulist, 1984), 61.

3. Ibid., 65.

4. Abraham Joshua Heschel, *The Sabbath: Its Meaning for Modern Man* (New York: Farrar, Straus and Giroux, 1984), 8.

5. Ibid., 10.

6. Ibid., 82.

7. Ibid., 97-101.

8. Steindl-Rast, *Gratefulness: The Heart of Prayer,* 69ff.

9. M. Scott Peck, *The Road Less Traveled* (New York: Simon and Shuster, 1978), 307-312.

## Chapter Five

1. Ched Myers, *Binding the Strongman: A Political Reading of Mark's Story of Jesus* (New York: Orbis Books, 1988), 281-289.

## Chapter Seven

1. From a letter to the congregation at Gladwyne Presbyterian Church, October 4, 1984.

## Chapter Eight

1. Charles M. Olsen, *Transforming Church Boards into Communities of Spiritual Leaders* (Washington, D.C.: Alban Institute Press, 1995).

2. Spiritual centers that offer training in spiritual direction include: Oasis Ministries, Camp Hill, Pennsylvania; Shalem Institute, Washington, D.C.; Wainwright House, Rye, New York; Listening Hearts Ministries, Baltimore, Maryland. Resources for spiritual growth I have found helpful include: Elizabeth O'Connor, *Journey Inward, Journey Outward* (New York: Harper and Row, 1968), and *Search for Silence* (San Diego: Lura-Media, 1986); Brother Lawrence, *The Practice of the Presence of God* (Washington, D.C.: Institute of Carmelite Studies, 1994); Richard J. Foster, *Freedom of Simplicity* (New York: Harper and Row, 1981), and *Celebration of Discipline: The Path to Spiritual Growth* (New York: Harper and Row, 1978); Emilie Griffin, *Clinging: The Experience of Prayer* (New York: Harper and Row, 1984); Morton T. Kelsey, *Companions on the Inner Way: The Art of Spiritual Guidance* (New York: Crossroads, 1983); Anthony deMello, *Sadhana: A Way to God* (St. Louis, The Institute of Jesuit Sources, 1978); William McNamara, *The Human Adventure: Contemplation for Everyman* (New York: Doubleday and Company, 1974); Thich Nhat Hanh, *Peace Is Every Step: The Path of Mindfulness in Everyday Life* (New York: Bantam Books, 1991); Tilden Edwards, *Living in the Presence: Disciplines for the Spiritual Heart* (San Francisco; Harper, 1987); Maria Harris, *Dance of the Spirit: The Seven Steps of Women's Spirituality* (New York: Bantam Books, 1991); any of the *Meditations With* series (Santa Fe: Bear and Company); virtually any book by Henri J. M. Nouwen; and all the other books referred to in this book.

3. Parker J. Palmer, "Borne Again: The Monastic Way to Church Renewal," in *The Auburn News*, Fall 1985, 5.

4. Marilyn Ferguson, *The Aquarian Conspiracy: Personal and Social Transformation in the 1980's* (Los Angeles: J. P. Tarcher, Inc., 1980), 157-167.

5. Matthew Fox, from a lecture/workshop sponsored by Gladwyne Presbyterian Church, October 17, 1991.

## Chapter Ten

1. See Stephen R. Covey, *Principle-Centered Leadership* (New York: Simon and Shuster, 1990), 137, 194-195, 210-216, and Marvin Weisbord, *Discovering Common Ground*, 71–124. I learned the specific phrases "self-directed people" and "self-managed teams" at a FutureSearch Workshop, American College of Underwriters, April 1995, led by Marvin Weisbord and Sandra Janov.

## Chapter Eleven

1. Reinhold Niebuhr, *The Nature and Destiny of Man* (New York: Charles Scribner's Sons, 1941), I:112-122, 164-166; II:47-52, 287-321.

2. Gilbert Rendle, "Managing Change in the Church," a presentation at an Alban Institute Workshop, October 3-5, 1995, Bon Secours Center, Marriotsville, Maryland.

3. Roy Morrison, *We Build the Road As We Go* (Philadelphia: New Society Publishers, 1991), 28-32, 222-223.

## Conclusion

1. Albert Nolan, "Four Stages of Spiritual Growth in Helping the Poor," *Praying*, P.O. Box 410335, Kansas City, MO 64141. This article is part of the reentry packet for participants in groups at the Cuernavaca Center for Intercultural Dialogue on Development, Cuernavaca, Mexico.

what do you want?
what do you long for?
what do you yearn for?
then in context of Church!
p28- questions #1/#2.
remind of any scripture?